A truly hopeful, practical, humble, real, and empowering book about partnering with God to see the kingdom come. If you want to do good in the world but feel overwhelmed, I'm so happy to hand this book to you with my highest confidence that it will matter in you and through you. I've worked with Chris for years now and he's the real deal.

Sarah Bessey, author of *Jesus Feminist* and
*Out of Sorts: Making Peace with an Evolving Faith*

Too busy to get involved? Feeling ill-equipped? Chris's *Doing Good Is Simple* answers those excuses and more by proving that God can use anything—even lemonade, whistles, and garage sales—if we "have a willing heart and a clear understanding" of why we exist. This must-read book proves that lives are saved when we get creative, have a little fun, and adjust our thinking.

Adam LaRoche, retired baseball player and abolitionist

Sometimes you read books about the difficulties in this world, the extreme poverty, the millions of orphans, and the slavery that still exists, and you know there are things you need to know, but when you put the book down you feel nothing but sadness and helplessness. This is not one of those books. While *Doing Good Is Simple* gives you some hard truths, from the very beginning the overwhelming feeling is one of hope. You finish reading knowing that there is absolutely something you can do to combat the evils in this world. There is most definitely a way you can be a part of the solution. I've had the privilege of traveling with Chris Marlow and have seen firsthand the lives Help One Now is saving with the help of many everyday normal people like you and me. What he is saying is true. We are called to do good in this world, and it's not as hard as you might think.

Korie Robertson, author of *Strong and Kind*
and star of A&E's *Duck Dynasty*

So many times, we think we have to have a lot of money, influence, and time in order to make a big impact. In *Doing Good Is Simple*, Chris Marlow flips that belief on its head and shows you that making a difference really can be simple. His book and the stories in it will inspire you to start doing good right where you are with the time and resources you have!

Crystal Paine, founder of MoneySavingMom.com
and *New York Times* bestselling author

Most of us want to do good. But the fear of doing it the wrong way often keeps us from doing anything at all. *Doing Good Is Simple* is full of stories, biblical insight, and true-life experiences that inform, equip, and empower us to live a life of compassion. It's a much-needed read by a man who knows what he's talking about.

Brandon Hatmaker, Founder of the Legacy Collective;
author of *Barefoot Church* and *A Mile Wide*

If you want to start a movement, read this book. If you want to live a better, more fulfilled life, read this book. If you doubt such a life is even possible, read this book. Chris is right: Doing good *is* simple. And through approachable but powerful stories, he guides you through a process that will change your life, your community, and maybe even your world.

Jeff Goins, bestselling author of *The Art of Work*

With so many opportunities to "do good" in modern society, the call to philanthropy can leave us feeling weighed down and worn out. Luckily, as Chris Marlow says, it isn't as difficult as it appears. Transforming your life into a force for social change is as easy as squeezing lemons or opening a garage door. If trying to be "good" has left you feeling burned out, beat up, or bewildered, this book is for you!

Jonathan Merritt, author of *Jesus Is Better Than You Imagined*
and contributing writer for *The Atlantic*

I'm so grateful for Chris Marlow, his radical vision, and humble example—showing me how to better love and serve my neighbor. His book *Doing Good Is Simple* is built on years of hard experience and relational authority—and it calls us to see and love the person right in front of us.

Dr. John Sowers, President, The Mentoring Project

Chris Marlow is a bridge builder who made inviting my blog readers to do good in South Africa simple. What I thought would be hard and complicated, Chris and Help One Now made easy. Thousands of moms rallied around one simple project that resulted in a community water point, vegetable garden, playground, and classrooms. No mega donors, just many small amounts given by readers right in the middle of their everyday lives.

Lisa-Jo Baker, author of *Surprised by Motherhood* and community manager for (in)courage

*Doing Good Is Simple* is refreshingly honest, unpretentious, and filled with life-shaping insights that will inspire you to do good. Chris reminds us of the collective power of simple actions that truly do make a world of difference. Read this book and get ready to participate.

Charles Lee, CEO of !deation and author of *Good Idea. Now What?*

Overwhelmed by the needs around you? *Doing Good Is Simple* will help you cut through the fog with a clear path towards making an impact with whatever background, experience, or resources you have.

Mike Rusch, CEO, Pure Charity

Words can't express the commitment Chris has shown with his life's actions, but this book will give words to how we might join him in action!

Jeff Shinabarger, Founder of Plywood People and author of *More or Less: Choosing a Lifestyle of Generosity*

# Doing Good Is Simple

# Doing Good Is Simple

CHRIS MARLOW

ZONDERVAN

*Doing Good Is Simple*
Copyright © 2016 by Chris Marlow

Requests for information should be addressed to:
Zondervan, 3900 Sparks Dr. SE, Grand Rapids, Michigan 49546

ISBN 978-0-310-34361-5 (ebook)

Library of Congress Cataloging-in-Publication Data

Names: Marlow, Chris, 1973- author.
Title: Doing good is simple : making a difference right where you are / Chris
    Marlow.
Description: Grand Rapids : Zondervan, 2016.
Identifiers: LCCN 2016000227 | ISBN 9780310343578 (softcover)
Subjects: LCSH: Christian life. | Helping behavior—Religious aspects—
    Christianity. | Change—Religious aspects—Christianity.
Classification: LCC BV4501.3 .M268 2016 | DDC 248.4—dc23 LC record
    available at https://lccn.loc.gov/2016000227

Published in association with Christopher Ferebee.

*Cover design: Curt Diepenhorst*
*Cover photo: © belindaroberts / Getty Images®*
*Interior design: Kait Lamphere*

First printing June 2016 / Printed in the United States of America

This book is for:

My three favorite people in the world—

Necole, Bailey, and Mackenzie;

the Help One Now board, staff and tribe—

I'm thankful for all the hard work, sacrifice, and commitment;

you make the world brighter through the lives that you live;

and our local leaders,

who are the real heroes of this story—

you help us see the powerful results of doing good

# Contents

# Foreword

I took my first trip to another country when I was in high school, and my contribution to a vulnerable community was a truly subpar painting job of a building that didn't need paint. I also engaged children and locals at a time when I had exactly zero understanding of their culture, struggles, felt needs, and traditions—which didn't stop me from barreling in with spiritual counsel because who wouldn't want advice from a sixteen-year-old cheerleader from Kansas?

Later, as my husband, Brandon, and I led student ministry, we led trips that had about the same "positive" impact. When I think back on the hosting missionaries that put up with our ignorance and foolishness, I want to go back and give them ten million dollars for their restraint. I cannot imagine why they agreed to host twenty-five Midwestern teenagers with an evangelical hero complex, but they certainly deserve to be rewarded for their longsuffering.

Now, twenty years later, I can tell you this with sincerity: Almost everything I've learned about engaging vulnerable communities with respect and integrity, I learned from Chris Marlow and Help One Now. Until I began partnering with their work in 2009, I didn't even know what I didn't know. I had never seen another way, an alternative to the "experiential short-term mission trip," a more intelligent approach to international community development. I came alongside HON first as a quiet learner, then a participant, then an influencer, and now a full-blown proselytizer. I drank every drop of their Kool-Aid, and I'll tell you what: I'm buying what they are selling.

I've learned this from Chris and the HON model: Let's start where we should always start: the local community we wish to serve, whether international or domestic. This should not be an afterthought to our trip details. No community is an agenda, an outlet, or a lesson, and its people are not photo ops. Poor people are not dumb, clueless, helpless, or ignorant; they are resourceful and resilient. Any wrong thinking that casts them as folks to pity and fix needs eradicating. We do not start with our trip; we start with the people.

*Anytime the rich and poor combine, we should listen to whoever has the least power.* Rich people are conditioned to assess the world through our privilege. The powerful tend to discredit or ignore the marginalized perspective because we can. We are shielded from the effects of a lopsided equation; we reap the benefits, not the losses. We don't mean to do this (or even know we are doing it), but we evaluate other communities through the lens of advantage, assuming we know best, have the most to offer. In doing so, we unintentionally elevate our perception.

Every missional conversation should begin with local leaders, local families, local ministries, and the local perspective. *Tell us about your community. What is the history? What have you overcome?*

*What are you still battling? How are you leading your people? What has worked? What has failed? What is the local vision for community development? Who else is leading well? How is the partnership with your government? What systems are broken in your community? What is your greatest need right now? What is your greatest strength to that end? Where is God moving? How we can support what you are already doing? How could we best serve you? What "help" has actually hurt, and how can we avoid that? Is a short-term team of any value to you, or could we better partner from afar?*

Having traveled on many international HON trips and served as a board member for the last two years, I can assure you: this is precisely how Chris and his team engage the communities they serve. We have such high-capacity local leaders in the countries we work in, it would blow your mind. They are easily the best visionaries I've ever been exposed to, and we follow their leadership at every turn.

Help One Now is fiercely committed to helping and not hurting, and Chris has led with that nonnegotiable firmly in place since day one. He is a trustworthy leader, a courageous freedom fighter, a creative thinker, and a true brother. If Chris embodies the next generation of community developers, the world will soon be safer, stronger, and more beautiful for the vulnerable. He is a champion for the poor, and it is such an honor to be his partner and friend in this good work. I hope you'll join him in this journey of believing that doing good truly is simple, and letting him be your guide as you live it out.

*Jen Hatmaker*

# Introduction: Good Grief

A life interrupted is a life inspired.
Greg Russinger

Dust billowed from behind our van's tires, and the fear and exhaustion inside the vehicle was palpable, heavy. Zimbabwe was one of the most dangerous countries in the world at the time and teetering on the brink of civil war. The US State Department told travelers not to enter its borders, and those who did would be on their own. We had no choice but to disregard their warnings.

It was four o'clock in the morning, and our group—a local pastor and his wife, a missionary friend from North Carolina, me, and three other people from my Texas church—had been driving nonstop for more than twenty hours. The ride had been nothing short of a roller coaster. Cows attempted to cross the road without warning, rickety busses traveling 100 kmph whizzed past with only inches to spare, and Zimbabwean security checkpoints popped up every hour or so, asking us where we were going and why. The tension in the van was thick as smoke. One of our team members wept in the back, overwhelmed by what we had experienced so far. We had reached a breaking point.

A question shattered the stillness: "Chris, do you mind if we stop for a second at a gas station up the road? I need to check on some kids."

Pastor John's query seemed simple on the surface, and I had no reason to distrust him. We met him and his wife, Orpha, on the border of South Africa hours earlier. They loaded our twelve-passenger van with supplies for the orphans for whom they were caring. But the question filled me with anxiety because of *where* it was asked.

Zimbabwe was not the kind of place you wanted to pull over in the middle of the night. When we crossed the border, police officers warned us to stop only if we absolutely had to. The country was desperate for international assistance, starvation was becoming the norm, and the majority of the country lacked electrical power most of the time. To feed their children, parents resorted to robbing travelers along the freeway. Pulling over at a dark gas station was one of the last items on my list of good ideas right now.

"John, it's four in the morning, and we're all very tired," I said, trying to hide my frustration. "Do you really think it's a good idea to stop?"

John, a humble man, never broke eye contact. The tone of his voice was graceful but authoritative: "Chris, I need to check on these children. It will only take a moment. Can we please stop?"

The contrast was clear: I was a pastor from Austin, Texas, who had never traveled further than Mexico. The day's journey had left me exhausted and fearful. Meanwhile, John was a Spirit-filled visionary who was not going to let the matter rest.

It was settled. Our van—filled with food, water, gasoline, and a team of people who were unmistakably foreign—pulled into an abandoned gas station in Harare, Zimbabwe, in the middle of the night.

When our van ground to a halt and the dust settled, the headlights illuminated the gas station's interior. Dozens of children—orphans—were lying on the cold concrete floor, huddled together for warmth, protection, and some shred of belonging. I struggled to catch my breath.

The kids slowly woke, letting their eyes adjust to the sudden burst of light. As our team—including five white Americans—climbed out of the van, confusion reigned. *Have they come to bring food? Water? Maybe to rescue us from this bankrupt, broken country?*

The children instantly surrounded me, clinging to my arms and legs and tugging at my clothing. I felt trapped; it was a scene reminiscent of the news reports of Michael Jackson walking the streets of London, suffocated by a sea of fans. My arms were weighed down by hanging children, and my shirt felt like it would be ripped from my back.

That's when it happened, all in one instant—really, half of an instant. A boy, no more than eight years old, with a determined brow and crust around his mouth, gripped my hand with authority. His brown eyes paralyzed me, and I was unable to resist as he pulled me low. The rest of the children grew nearly silent, signaling that this young man was a dominant figure in this makeshift community.

*"Sir, thank you for visiting my country. I'm so sorry it's in the*

*shape that it's in,"* he said. *"I don't want to beg you for food, but I have not had anything to eat in days. Is there anything I can do to work for you, so I can get something to eat?"*

Nothing in my life had prepared me for his question, and my tongue tripped over my answer.

"No. I have nothing for you, and I'm sorry."

He was crushed. They were all crushed. And now I was crushed too.

The truth was not on my side. In South Africa earlier that day, we filled the van full of food for the thirty orphans John and Orpha were providing for.

I also had access to other resources, such as a pocket full of money and a backpack full of snacks, but I froze. No one told me how to handle this kind of situation, and the weight of the moment threw me off.

This child was helpless and hopeless; he was close to starving. He was made in the image of God. He asked for help, and I turned him away . . . without excuse. I felt as if I had betrayed the gospel, like I had looked a needy Jesus in the face and turned him away. I only had bad news for that boy.

We crawled back into the van and drove in silence. Tears rolled down my face against my will. I wished more than anything I had responded differently. I could have done something—anything— *what was wrong with me?* Within the hour we arrived at Pastor John's home for a quick nap. I slept fitfully. How could I not?

Later that day we reached our destination—Pastor John's orphanage. We took this trip to visit these thirty kids and hopefully determine a way to help them. We had an entire day to spend with them, and I often had to slip away to compose myself. Their stories tore at my heart. One child told me her parents abandoned her at a local hospital because they could not afford to feed her. Another recalled being left at a local garbage dump and being forced to search for food amid the trash to avoid starvation.

"Pastor John, how long will these supplies last?" I asked as we unloaded the van.

He paused to survey the provisions. His eyes darted as he calculated the horrible answer: "Three weeks, I suppose."

"Pastor, what will you do when you run out?" I asked.

"I'm not sure, but I know that now I don't have to worry about providing for these kids for the next three weeks," Pastor John said. "That's a long time, and I know God always provides. So don't worry, Chris."

Silence.

My anger toward God and myself thickened. I could not understand how God could let his children live like this, and I hated myself for my own inaction.

A few minutes at a gas station and a single day with thirty orphans changed my life. It was as if God had pried me out of my comfortable Western Christian context, dropped me in the middle of hell, slapped me in the face, and shouted, "Wake up! I need you to care for these little ones *because I do*." This was the mission God had given me, had given us, and I had ignored it for nearly two decades.

My life had been forever interrupted.

# From Interruption to Inspiration

Six years before I arrived in Zimbabwe, my soul began stirring. I was pastoring a church plant with my friends Jasen and Ken. During a staff meeting in a local coffeehouse, we asked ourselves, "How could God use our little church to care for the poor in our city—Raleigh—and the world?"

Unfortunately, life intervened, and two years later we closed our church and parted ways. I moved to Austin, Ken to Seattle, and Jasen to California.

I couldn't shake the stirring I'd felt. I began to read the Bible anew. Themes emerged that I had somehow overlooked, and a single message reverberated from its pages: *God cares for the poor, widows, and orphans. If God cares, I should too.*

Perhaps like you, my own sense of insufficiency neutralized my desire to do something about those in need. What can I do? I'm just a normal person with a wife, two daughters, a mortgage, school loans, and a suburban lifestyle. God kept drawing me toward a greater mission—to do good in the world—but I found myself too busy and feeling too ill equipped to respond. Simple, day-to-day responsibilities like carpooling, grocery shopping, caring for my girls, and my working suddenly seemed overwhelming.

But when we fail to act, God often acts on our behalf.

I was watching ESPN and waiting for dinner to be served at my mother-in-law's home one night and decided to go through some mail I'd picked up at my church office. I decided to watch the *Invisible Children* DVD that was in the middle of the stack.

The twelve-minute film told the story of Emmy, a poor boy whose mother had AIDS. It felt like heaven descended on the room as I watched. By the time the credits rolled, my eyes were wet. Embarrassed by my tears, I slipped away to the only private place available—the bathroom, which, of course, was shared with a cat and her litter box. This was not the ideal place, but God does not care about where we meet him. God cares about whether we come when he calls. I fell to my knees, and the porcelain throne became a holy altar.

*God, forgive me for my lack of action. Break my heart with what breaks your heart.*

A little research in the following week told me that kids like Emmy die every six seconds.[1] Meanwhile, pastors like me spend twenty hours each week preparing Christmas and Easter sermons and thinking about how to raise funds for another building project. My "job" as a pastor made me too busy for the Emmys of the world.

In the midst of this research, I realized the old adage was true: you must be careful what you pray for, because you just might get it. Little did I know, God was about to give me an opportunity to travel to Zimbabwe where he could shake me awake, and this time "no" would not be an option.

# A Long Way Home

On the thirty-hour trip from Zimbabwe to Austin, I took out a Bible and my journal and scribbled down all the verses I'd been stumbling across in the months prior. Among the most compelling were:

- "He defends the cause of the fatherless and the widow, and loves the foreigner residing among you, giving them food and clothing." (Deuteronomy 10:18)
- A father to the fatherless, a defender of widows, is God in his holy dwelling. (Psalm 68:5)
- "Learn to do right; seek justice. Defend the oppressed. Take up the cause of the fatherless; plead the case of the widow." (Isaiah 1:17)
- "[At judgment,] the King will say to those on his right, 'Come, you who are blessed by my Father; take your inheritance, the kingdom prepared for you since the creation of the world. For I was hungry and you gave me something to eat, I was thirsty and you gave me something to drink, I was a stranger and you invited me in, I needed clothes and you clothed me, I was sick and you looked after me, I was in prison and you came to visit me.'" (Matthew 25:34–36)
- Religion that God our father accepts as pure and faultless is this: to look after orphans and widows in their distress and to keep oneself from being polluted by the world. (James 1:27)

An unbroken thread woven throughout Scripture shouted God's love for those in need and called us to care for, defend, and bless them. How had I missed this for so long?

When the plane landed, I had made up my mind that I was going to devote the next portion of my life to *doing* good and not just talking about it.

Maybe you've found yourself in a similar situation. You glimpsed a sponsored child's picture on a friend's fridge and haven't been able to shake the image from your mind. Or you took a trip overseas and woke to the reality that the world is a lot bigger than your suburban neighborhood. Or maybe you've had a creeping feeling that you want your family's life to consist of more than just soccer practices and PTA meetings and working overtime. As these emotions stir, you begin to feel like I do— that we were meant for more than our routines, hobbies, and job descriptions.

Or you've struggled with the weight of guilt and shame or have become overwhelmed by compassion fatigue. So many problems and so many ways to help can often paralyze us. Doing good turns into a hassle, and then we just stop and ignore it all. Our apathy turns into guilt, and we've basically created a vortex that wounds our own souls and hurts those who need our help.

*This is not the way of Jesus.* He calls us to love and to serve, reminding us that love and service create joy and fill our souls with peace. He inspires us to do good, and do it well.

If that's you, I have some good news: doing good is not as difficult as you assumed. It's not as complicated as you thought or as taxing as you supposed. It won't require moving to Africa or giving up all your modern comforts or burdening your already overwhelmed family. But it *will* require you to get creative, have a little fun, and shift some of your thinking.

It really is that simple.

# Lemonade with a Purpose

## *How to Start Small Wherever You Are*

Never doubt that a small group of thoughtful,
committed citizens can change the world;
indeed, it's the only thing that ever has.

**Margaret Mead**

Sometimes you go searching for your calling in life. Other times, your calling comes searching for you. I learned that lesson in Zimbabwe. Never in a million years would I have thought that I would be doing what I'm doing!

How we respond to moments of interruption determines who we become and how we spend our lives. But you can never fully live in your calling without going through struggle, fear, and failure. Our decisions in those moments determine the legacy we will leave.

# Fighting Normal

How long did it take for life to feel normal again after I returned from Zimbabwe?

*Ninety days.*

Memories slowly faded. Routine crept back in. Life returned to its usual pace. Taking the kids to school, a never-ending list of household chores, and a couple visits to my favorite Austin taco stand hastened the transition back to normalcy.

Even still, I remained haunted by my experience in that desperate African country. I felt that being pulled between the demands of my life in Austin and the orphans I wanted to help halfway around the world would tear me apart.

Right before I left the orphanage, I dragged my heavy heart to the entrance gate. Dozens of kids outside the compound ran to talk to me. A piece of slatted sheet metal separated us. Behind me, gravel crunched as Pastor John came to comfort me. Throwing his arm around my shoulder, he pulled me tight. He knew the experience had overwhelmed me.

A girl outside the gates of the orphanage shouted in: "Pastor John, do you have any beds available yet?"

The seasoned minister knelt down in the dirt and peered through the gate. Compassion saturated his words: "No. I'm sorry. We have no more beds."

Pastor John explained to me later that these were community orphans. They roamed the town with no place to live. At night most slept in the bush or at a park or perhaps a church. They were without homes or families, and there weren't adequate resources to help them.

I thought of my two daughters—five and seven at the time—waiting for me back in Austin. What if something happened to my wife and me? What if they were left without a home and a family? What if the social infrastructure wasn't in place to care for them? I couldn't imagine these two girls whom I loved more than my own life being driven into the streets.

In that moment, I felt I'd glimpsed God's heart. *How must our heavenly Father feel about millions of his children sleeping in streets and abandoned parks? If his heart is broken, shouldn't mine be too? And shouldn't that broken heart lead me to act?*

I recalled verses like Psalm 68:6, which teaches that God places the lonely in families. The children behind the sheet metal divider needed a family. Church leaders in Zimbabwe were prepared to fill the gap, but they could barely afford to care for their own children.

That's when a question popped into my head that would return to haunt me, even in those first ninety days after having returned to my American comfort: *What if regular people around the globe partnered to empower Zimbabwean leaders to care for their community's orphans?*

I had found my mission.

# Three Hurdles to Doing Good

I returned home determined to fight global poverty beginning with the orphans I met in Zimbabwe, but I didn't know anything about the problem or its potential solutions. I spent my early mornings and late nights poring over Scripture and everything on extreme poverty I could get my hands on, including books like *Walking with the Poor* and *When Helping Hurts.*

I soon swam in a sea of information—complicated, convoluted, and sometimes conflicting—about sponsorships, adoption, microloans, water projects, and job creation. These thoughtful authors all had different ideas on how to do good and do it well. Some instructed their readers never to go on a mission trip again while others said, "You need to be on a plane tomorrow and experience the issues firsthand." One author concluded that adoption was terrible while others argued it was the best way to help the poor. My enthusiasm morphed into discouragement as I ran headlong into three hurdles for doing good.

## Hurdle #1: "The Issues Are Too Numerous"

I discovered that orphan care and global poverty connected to other issues. Each one was equally concerning, equally in need of advocacy, equally massive in scale. Environmental devastation, child soldiers, global hunger, malaria outbreaks, genital mutilation, lack of healthcare, inadequate schools, clean water shortages, the oppression of women. The spiderweb of global problems entangled me like a housefly.

I'd always known that disease and devastation permeated the world, but Zimbabwe made that knowledge more meaningful. These were no longer issues "over there." The numbers became names and faces and families. They were broken dreams and broken hearts.

But how could I possibly choose between so many noble and pressing causes?

The sheer number of problems paralyzed me and bred cynicism in my heart. If the issues were too big and too numerous, maybe I should ignore them all. The whole experience left me feeling small and helpless and angry. Even if I donated every penny in my savings account and every hour in my day, I wouldn't be able to make a dent in the sum total of the world's troubles.

## Hurdle #2: "The Problems Are Too Big"

In 2010, about 2.4 billion people lived on less than 2 USD per day.[1] For those of us who want to do good in the world, this number feels like a stone wall. How can one person—or even one family—hope to even chip away at such a mammoth number?

Even when I considered only the global orphan crisis, I discovered that some organizations estimated as many as 140 million orphans worldwide. This number was hardly more manageable. The more I researched global issues, the more I wanted to ignore them all. I had enough stress, fear, worry, and obligations in life. Why should I commit my life to problems too big to solve?

## Hurdle #3: "The Solutions Are Too Complicated"

Sometimes solutions are simpler than problems. Maybe reading some books from experts on how to solve these global issues holistically would give me hope. Perhaps there was a silver bullet.

No. The more I read, the more my spirit sank. Every expert presented a different solution, and every solution was more complex than the last. Was the solution government action or nonprofit engagement or changing individual behaviors? Depends on whom you ask. Worse still, many proposed solutions conflicted with each other. Without a PhD in political science or economics or international relations—or all three—I didn't feel qualified to discern which was best.

The three hurdles combined didn't just trip me up. They left me—like so many others who begin to research what doing good means for them—flat on my face. The search drained me, and I was beginning to believe the whole endeavor was a lost and doomed cause.

My memories of Zimbabwe faded a little more with each passing day—a stamp on my passport, some pictures on Facebook, a story or two, but little more—and my passion waned. I soon began entertaining excuses in my mind. *I'm too busy. I need to care for my own family. I'll never accomplish anything anyway.* I was teetering on surrender.

I discovered that compassion fatigue is a real thing. Emotions, so strong at first, can easily shift into apathy. The subsequent guilt is paralyzing; it can prevent us from ever doing anything and freeze us into inaction. No wonder some people live for themselves, unaware of or unengaged with those who desperately need help. *When global problems overwhelm, the human tendency is to do nothing.*

# Jumping over the Hurdles

Have you ever wanted to change something but never could? Maybe you tried to lose weight, eat better, quit smoking, go back to school, or save money, but as you planned your steps, you got mired in the details and never moved. If you've been there, you too have experienced the paralysis of analysis. In a moment of overwhelming resistance, you have a choice: lose heart and quit or simplify the process.

I was tempted to stop caring and embrace apathy. But I knew the kids I met deserved my best efforts to figure it out. Plus, I wondered, "Why would Scripture speak so clearly if normal people weren't equipped to do good?"

I knew that if I wanted to impact these kids in Zimbabwe, I desperately needed to *simplify the complicated* and give people a clear and powerful way to help. Jesus used a handful of untrained fishermen to change the world. Those men did not have PhDs in theology or credentials to impress the powers that be. No doubt Jesus is still using everyday, normal people who take simple yet significant steps to do good.

I decided to press forward and focus on overcoming the hurdles, and in the process I discovered six key things to help direct my energy.

## 1. Do Something Rather than Nothing

I was having dinner with my friend Alan, who has written several books on missiology. Alan noted that Christians historically have been a people of action. I wrestled with that thought because I want to make sure this current generation of Christians upheld that mantle. Yet I fear that if we are not careful, we will be known more for our social media rants and our comfortable church-service experiences. We sing and preach about justice, compassion, and mercy, yet our lives are disconnected from these outcomes in the real world. We must have the conviction to take an action; we must do something.

## 2. Start Small

You don't have to start with a big check or a year-long commitment. You don't have to try to save the world; that is not your burden. But you do have to start. Take a small step in the direction of action and justice-seeking. At Help One Now, we have multiple ways to get involved, such as the *Ten Dollar Tribe*. My author friends Lisa-Jo Baker and Crystal Paine took a trip to South Africa, where they spent time with kids who were vulnerable or orphaned. They wanted to help give these kids a future, so they encouraged their readers to get involved. Over the course of two days, they inspired over 150 people to join the *Ten Dollar Tribe*–South Africa. Each month, we use those funds to make a difference. Tribe members give just $10 a month— something like two lattes—and real lives are changed. We did this so people would have a small, simple way to help, to take action, to start somewhere, and collectively make a big impact.

## 3. Follow Your Passions

What motivates you? What keeps you up at night? What do you love to do? Try to connect your passions in life with doing good. If you love education, get involved with an educational nonprofit. If you love job creation or healthcare, find simple ways to get involved with causes that are trying to solve those problems. If you love fashion, get involved with artisan groups. You can define and shape how you get involved and take action.

## 4. Use Your Gifts

Simply writing checks will no longer suffice. Many people want to do more, to get their hands dirty; they want to be involved and feel connected. Why? Because we are gifted. When we connect our gifts with focused outcomes, we see amazing progress.

I run a nonprofit. It takes money to accomplish the mission—I make no bones about that. But it also takes human capital. We have a CFO that we could never afford to pay at this stage in our organization, but this man, who is semiretired and in his fifties, uses his gifts to help us be financially disciplined. We understand the data and we're able to make much better choices, which then create a much greater impact. We also have folks who use their gifts in the countries we serve. They train teachers, help solve water problems, or teach theology and business. These action-oriented women and men are on the frontlines doing work that matters. And they love it! It brings life to them as they help bring life to others.

## 5. Build Relationships

I'm a big fan of commitment. Popping into a country, doing a service project, and popping out will not make the impact necessary to see lasting change. Again, doing good is so much more than a seven-day trip or the occasional check. It's hard to make a real impact if you're not connected to real people. I can't tell you how many times I have listened to stories from people who went on a mission trip. They talk about what they did as opposed to who they met.

"We painted an orphanage . . . we led a sports camp . . . we did a VBS." Yet, often, they don't actually connect with the people they're serving. They don't know their stories; they did not take time to listen and learn. When we spend time with people, especially those who live in extreme poverty, and we listen to their stories, it creates dignity and connectedness—something they usually lack.

I was in the Dominican Republic with my friend Korie and her family. They've been caring for a group of fourteen orphans for ten years. Their interactions with the kids were amazing. This was not a service project (though they did serve); this was a time to reconnect with kids to whom they have been committed—kids they know and love. The conversations were about the next ten years and how they could help these kids become amazing adults.

They knew their stories, they knew their hopes and dreams, and they cared for these kids as if they were their own.

We all want to know and be known. That's why doing good is so powerful when the focus is first and foremost the people and not the project.

## 6. Stick With It

The older you grow, the more you know. I've realized that those who are truly changing the world, on both a small and large scale, do hard work for a long time. These people chose the path filled with commitment, they have courage to stay the course and not be fickle, and they desire to dig deep and see real progress.

Because of constant change in my life or due to things beyond my control, I always struggled to follow through on key commitments. I wanted to be faithful, yet that required more of me than I was willing to offer. When work would get hard, I would quit and move on. When conflict would arise, I would avoid it and bail out. When failure took place, instead of helping, I would go on to the next thing.

And then I realized that conflict is a constant; I had to deal with it. Hard work is a gift from God; it's hard to stick with it, but when you do, you get to see true progress and real results.

One of our larger donors told me that if we are not failing, we are not trying hard enough. His permission to be human empowered me as a young nonprofit leader to take risks, because I knew he would stick with me. His and his family's commitment and support have helped me focus on building an organization that lasts and makes an impact far beyond both of our lives.

Folks who make a true difference are not concerned about the "new hip thing." They find people they love, respect, trust, and those folks stay on course (which is absolutely vital if you want to make an impact). It takes hard work, focus, and discipline, but when you partner with key causes and key people and work together for years, you will see what few ever get to see—real progress!

## Coffee, Lemonade, and a Couple of Tunes

Texas in the summer is hotter than the sun's surface. Like, fry-an-egg-on-the-sidewalk hot. And nothing is better on a summer day in Texas than lemonade . . . except maybe lemonade that accomplishes good. So my daughters decided to try a little front-yard entrepreneurship to raise money for the orphans in Zimbabwe.

The Friday night before we set up the lemonade stand, my daughters began drawing the tale of the orphans' stories on white poster board. Bailey and Mackenzie had never met the kids, but their stories had become important to them. The next morning we rose, dragged a table out to the sidewalk, taped up the poster board, and positioned a donation jar on top. They were the proudest lemonade stand operators west of the Mississippi.

Every quarter that jingled into the jar would light up my girls' eyes. As my neighbors sipped lemonade, they heard stories of the orphans we sought to help. Often that 25 cents became a $25 donation. The willingness of so many to contribute told me they wanted to do good but didn't know where to begin.

We raised $123 that day, which provided those thirty orphans with basic necessities—shelter, food, and water—for another few weeks. Moreover, we engaged in a positive activity that drew our family closer together. That night we counted our earnings and celebrated our accomplishment.

God provided for thirty children he loves just like that, using a couple of kids' imaginations and a few pitchers of lemonade.

Not to be shown up by my own daughters, this daddy devised his own plan. I decided to tap into Austin's famous music scene. A few of my musician friends agreed to play a live show at a local coffeehouse. The charity event, like most, was a gamble. I had no idea how many people would show up, but we told everyone we knew and crossed our fingers and toes. I smiled that night as nearly seventy people came to listen to music and support our cause.

Before the concert I took ten minutes to share the story of the children I'd met in Zimbabwe. People could donate if they wanted, and the coffee shop agreed to give 50 percent of their proceeds that night to the effort. In a blink we provided another three weeks of food for our children in Zimbabwe.

A few months later, I was having coffee with my friends Brandon and Jen Hatmaker. I shared my experience in Zimbabwe and how these kids had no clean water. They were forced to walk to the river each morning before school to fetch dirty water. They had no means of filtering water and no other supply. Desperate and exhausted, the kids at the orphanage held a fundraising rally in their own community to raise money for a new well so they wouldn't have to drink from where the animals bathed.

My friends' hearts broke with mine that morning. Brandon was a church planter who had just started Austin New Church. They decided to rally their people to raise enough money to fund a new clean water well for the orphans in Zimbabwe. Brandon sent out a call to address this need, and the people of Austin New Church responded. The small gifts added up, and we soon had enough money to build the well. Today clean water quenches the thirst of more than 130 orphans and the broader community.

Encouraged by our modest success, I shared these stories with everyone I knew. Through these conversations, a pattern emerged. Most people felt compassionate and wanted to do good in the world, but most of them didn't know what to do or how to start.

Most of my friends were as busy as I was. They juggled multiple first-world responsibilities—at work, at home, at church, in the community—and asking them to add a few more items to their to-do list failed to inspire them. They couldn't go work for UNICEF or World Vision. Maybe they could write a check or go on a short-term mission trip, sure, but we all knew this fell short of the call to *live* a good life.

I knew doing good couldn't be too difficult or complicated for average people. After all, God had asked *everyone* to care for those in need. And I had now experienced how simple acts can make a big difference.

As I began studying the most effective ways to engage global poverty and crises, I realized that doing good really *is* simple. A PhD in International Affairs isn't a prerequisite. You don't have to quit your job and join the Peace Corps or become a full-time volunteer. Some may, but most won't. And they don't need to.

By partnering in substantive ways with high-capacity indigenous leaders (like Pastor John and Orpha), regular people could create massive change in places of great need. I began to work with others to create easy tools and projects designed for CEO moms and stay-at-home dads, construction workers and entrepreneurs, brain surgeons and high school students.

As people saw they could do good while still having a life, they began recruiting others. And as more people began living good lives, I noticed that it had the added benefit of unifying families and communities. Brothers and sisters raised money to solve real problems, parents and children brainstormed small-scale community initiatives around the dinner table, husbands and wives created relationship-strengthening hobbies that improved the lives of others, friends would get together and deepen their bonds through service. Everything people feared they would need to give up was ironically improved by doing good together.

According to a recent study by Dr. Diana Garland,[2] kids who retained their Christian values as adults spent significant time serving together with their families. It's simply not enough to attend church or say bedtime prayers. Kids need to see their parents living out their faith, and they need to be invited to do the same at a young age.

A few small decisions led to a handful of donations collected from a few easy-to-execute projects. The result? Hundreds of lives were forever changed. I also began to see real-life benefits for parents who wanted to raise their kids to love their neighbor and serve people who are in need. We often hear what we need to do, but these real-life, frontline stories gave parents the opportunity to teach their kids what tangible love, sacrifice, and compassion meant.

## Simply Significant

Five years have passed since my family and I began planning projects like these, and we've seen those thirty children grow up into young men and women. Additionally, we've been able to rescue another 100 kids in that community. Dozens have been reunited with their families, and many are now adults who work jobs and are attending institutions of higher learning.

During my last visit to this community in Zimbabwe, I spent time with Deborah, the orphanage director. Walking the red dirt road, we passed houses the kids now call home, a playground brimming with laughter, and a community water well funded by Austin New Church.

Deborah paused.

"Thank you, Chris," she said in a somber tone. "If you and your partners had not been involved the last five years, many of these kids would have died."

I shivered at the thought. Doing good is *simple*, but it is also *significant*.

Who knew that coffee, lemonade, a few tunes, and a con-cerned church could transform the lives of children halfway around the world? And—perhaps equally astonishing—who knew it had the power to change the lives of our family and so many friends?

It's understandable if you're feeling a bit skeptical at this point. For modern Americans living in an advertising age and a culture of hype, the word *simple* might make you balk. The word makes us think "too good to be true" or "less than best." Thanks to the sharing of information in the twenty-first century, we're all painfully aware of the world's complexities. So when someone promises that something is both simple and significant, both easy and impactful, disbelief may tempt us.

But life is often far less complex than we make it.

A couple of kids selling lemonade, a few musicians playing some songs, a coffee shop owner donating a portion of his profit, a church funding a clean water well. Small steps *can* make a big difference. Intentional acts of kindness *can* transform communi-ties in need. A little creativity, a little collaboration, and a little time *can* transform lives.

Are you beginning to see how simple doing good can be?

—— 2 ——

# Ordinary Is the New Radical

*Because Jesus Doesn't Leave
Justice to the Professionals*

I have found that it is the small everyday
deeds of ordinary folks that keep the darkness
at bay. Small acts of kindness and love.

Gandalf (J. R. R. Tolkien, *The Hobbit*)

When I tucked my daughters into bed at night, I saw those kids on the other side of the world who lived on the other side of the gate. I would wonder what it was like for them to have no place to call home, no mom or dad to tuck them in. Every night my kids would find joy as they snuggled under the blankets, held their stuffed animals tightly, and rested in peace and safety.

When my family would sit around the dinner table, eat good food, laugh, and share stories of our day, my mind would often drift back to those kids in the gas station. They had no table, the stories they would share would not be filled with joy and laughter, they had no family and very little sense of belonging.

The words of William Wilberforce were so prescient: *"You may choose to look the other way but you can never say again that you did not know!"*[1] I realized I knew too much. I saw the palpable suffering, heard the tragic stories, but I also felt a mesmerizing sense of hope. God wanted to use normal people like my family to make a true difference in the world.

The timing could not have been worse. I was in my thirties, I had moved my family too many times, and I already had a failed church plant on my résumé. Our life was finally stable after years of chaos, and I did not want to do anything to disrupt my family! We were moving steadily toward the American dream. I had a dream job at Vista Community Church, my oldest daughter had just started school, and we had just purchased a home. Life was great.

But I've always known the American dream can be a gospel nightmare if it becomes an idol. If the American dream gets in the way of following God's call, it becomes like the millstone that hangs around our neck, causing us to drown (Matthew 18:6).

Of course, I'm still human. I felt compelled to act, but I was terrified to fail. For the first time in years, my family had a sense of security. Yet I knew I was about to blow it all up; I was going to trade our comfort for the chance to really make a change in the lives of children like the boy at the gas station. That boy, that grip, my words to him—it was just too much.

# Our New Normal

Doing good can be simple, but simple and easy are two different realities; we have to learn how to wrestle with that tension. Loving our neighbor will always cost us something. However, it will always give us something far better in return: a deep sense of worth. We ache for meaning and long for a life that matters, and I realized that I was discovering my purpose. This is vital, for neither families nor individuals can be healthy without a deep sense of meaning and mission.

You see, my little family chose to live for others; we wanted to become "others-focused." On the outside, not much had changed, but on the inside, a transformation was beginning to take shape. Is this not the call for the Christian, that we should live a life that is radically normal, a life that does not seem to make sense to most except for those who are following in the footsteps of Jesus? To live a life that reflects faith, hope, and love? To have a normal, but not *normal*, way of living?

We had seen the power of doing good. Real lives in the middle of Zimbabwe had vastly improved because our little family and small group of friends decided to be intentional and find ways to live more simply so that those thirty orphans could just live.

We wanted to do more. We wanted to help more. But that was going to cost us. As a family, we had to pick up our cross and take one step forward at a time; we had to learn to live more simply, to embrace the unknown future, and to exist in the chaos of the nonprofit world. This is what faith does. This is what it looks like to be a disciple of Jesus. It is beautiful and hard, and it requires faith, trust and sacrifice.

It's also for incredibly "normal" people, just like you and me.

# I Was an Orphan

Part of the reality of *doing good that is simple* is that you don't have to go to Zimbabwe to care for orphans. They are everywhere. I know, because I became one.

Like a lot of people, I was raised in a broken home. My mother was truly an amazing human, but she was terrible at relationships. For whatever reason, she thought the best place to meet a man was at the local biker bar—you know, the old-school joints that look and feel scary, with neon Bud Light signs, hairy men in patched leather vests, and tobacco smoke that fills the air and suffocates the lungs.

I never had the privilege of living the American dream, where a boy would watch football with his dad or go outside and play catch together. Usually I felt like a burden to all the men I was around.

As an eight-year-old kid, I had yet to meet my biological father, but I did have two temporary stepdads (which meant that my mom had three divorces on her résumé). I did not think much about my father; he never called, wrote, or sent any gifts for Christmas or birthdays. I also knew that my stepdads would only be around for a season before they moved on as well. Brokenness was normal.

My family was the typical 80s broken Gen-X family—two half sisters and two half brothers. Never in my lifetime did we all live together under one roof; we never spent Christmas together or went on any family vacations, and all of my siblings have struggled with crime, prison, and homelessness.

I struggled to find myself as a young person with no guide. In my early teens, my family life really began to deteriorate. My stepfather was abusive, my mother was diagnosed with cancer, and my siblings were all living on their own, in and out of jail.

My stepdad took his anger out on my mother. The only reason I stayed home and did not run away was to protect her, which often meant fistfights between him and me. The violence had gotten so bad that I would go to bed at night fully clothed, never knowing when I would need to defend my mother or myself.

One night I heard her screaming. My stepdad had decided to use my mother as a punching bag. Blood was everywhere, and my mother was crying and screaming for help.

I finally had enough. Punches were thrown, dishes were broken, and then I picked up a bar stool and swung it as hard as I could into my stepfather's head. He fell to the ground, and I summoned all my strength to pick up his drunken body and throw him through the window of his trailer. He fell hard on the concrete driveway as glass shattered everywhere.

When the police showed up, they arrested me, not knowing what had taken place. That night was the last straw, and my stepfather kicked me out and forced me to live on the streets. Thankfully, my brother was not in jail (for once), so I was able to crash at his place.

For spring break in high school one year, I headed down to San

Diego to party at the beach with some friends. We were antici-
pating a memory-making, epic week of fun in the sun, but my
dreams were dashed. After one night in San Diego, my friend's
dad's business back in Stockton burned down to the ground, so
we had to rush back home.

I was going to spend a week in San Diego, but all of a sudden
I was stuck in Stockton, which is in the northern California val-
ley. It is surrounded by farms and nowhere near the beach. My
amazing week had turned into a complete disaster. I was bored,
restless, and angry. I decided to page my close friend Vaughn
(using my pocketful of quarters and leaving the number to my
Motorola Bravo Plus) to find out what he was doing for the week.

He called me back, and I told him about my disaster in San
Diego. He said, "I'm going to camp in the mountains; want to
come?" Hmm, if I can't party on a beach, then I might as well go
to the Sierra Nevadas, right? Then he added the kicker: "Jennifer
is going to be there."

*Jennifer.*

Dang, I could spend an entire week camping with Jennifer?
My love, my lady (at least in my dreams). We sat next to each
other in history class (where I was a solid C student). I was in.

The following two days I went to church six times and to
evangelism classes twice—all the while barely comprehending
anything they were saying (Romans Road? WWJD? It was like
a secret code). But these crazy Christians were awesome. I had
never been around people with a genuine love for one another,
much less people who talked about a real God who wanted to

have a relationship with people. That was a foreign concept to me, and I had to wrestle through all the implications. Was God real? Did he love me?

On Wednesday night, after eating yet another meal of plastic chicken and macaroni and "cheese," we all gathered in the sanctuary for the evening service. I didn't know it yet, but I was about to encounter the living God. He was coming to rescue me.

Donnie Moore, the camp speaker, took the microphone again and began to talk. He shared these simple words: "God is a father to the fatherless. There are people here today who don't have fathers, but God wants to be your father, if you want that." And I did.

That night I became a follower of Jesus. *That night I was no longer an orphan. That night I found a Father who would not abandon me, a Father who would never abuse a woman, and a Father who was full of love, grace, and joy—three things I could barely recognize.*

## Rescued by Normal People

When I came home from camp to my brother's house, the first thing I saw was crime scene tape. My drug-dealing brother had been arrested and was off to prison again. My theology was weak and my understanding of evil was nil, but as I look back, surely the enemy was trying to destroy the seed that was planted at that camp.

I went to the nearest pay phone and called my mother to tell her what had happened at camp and that I had nowhere to live.

She invited me back home, but when I arrived to our trailer—the same spot where I threw my stepdad through a window—I would once again lose my family.

Seeing my stepfather for the first time in over a year was difficult. My mother told him I was a Christian now. I had no idea that he had a bad church experience and hated Christians—until he kicked me out of the house. Again.

It was Friday night, and after having the week of my life, I was homeless. Thankfully, my friend Vaughn picked up the phone when I called. Within the hour his mother picked me up as I was walking on the side of the road with all of my belongings in one backpack. They took me into their home for the weekend.

Soon they basically adopted me; I would move in with Vaughn's family for a year. It was this "normal" family that changed my life for good. Their church surrounded me with amazing community. They poured out so much love and helped me process all of my pain. I finally felt like I belonged.

I was not an easy kid to deal with, but they never gave up on me. For them, doing good was so simple: they just invited me to join their family.

Five years later, I was back in that trailer with my mother. Sadly, cancer was winning; she was on her deathbed. I remember holding her hand as she breathed her last breath and slipped into eternity. My mom was my hero. Even though life was rarely ever good, she really tried her best.

I never heard from my biological father again, and now my mother was no longer with me. But I was not an orphan because

I had a Father in God and a community in the local church. My life growing up was far from the American dream, but redemption won, light overcame the darkness, and good overcame evil because the church—God's people—did good by caring for me.

And that is how it is supposed to be.

Soon I would go to Bible college, become a youth pastor, and plant two churches. I married an amazing woman and we have two daughters. My life became tangible evidence that doing good is so vital. I cannot imagine what might have happened without Vaughn and his family, the youth group, and dozens of everyday, normal people who helped me in small and big ways. They were not superstars; they were the epitome of normal—a teacher, a plumber, a secretary, and a small-church youth pastor. God's people choose to live for others. When people allow God to use them in big and small ways, stories like mine can become the normal. These people taught me the invaluable lesson that everyday people can partner with God and change a broken kid's world.

They also gave me the confidence to believe that, twenty years later, we could start an organization and, if we did it right, have thousands of everyday normal people care for orphans around the world.

## The Most Powerful Mirror

When I got back from Zimbabwe, the Bible seemed brand new to me. I felt like that sixteen-year-old teenager, reading the Bible and experiencing God for the first time all over again. All the verses that talked about caring for the poor had a new sense of meaning. I began to relearn that the kingdom of God can be an amazing place when God's people are doing what they can to live out their faith tangibly.

In his epistle, James, the half brother of Jesus, communicates the need to do good with clarity, enthusiasm, and force. He begins his letter with the reminder that we will face trials (James 1:2). Then he tells the reader that if we lack wisdom, we can ask God, who gives it generously (1:5). He challenges us not to doubt but to have faith (1:6–8). He moves on to tell us to be quick to listen and slow to speak (1:19), and then he pens a very important piece of Scripture.

James throws down the gauntlet and draws a line in the sand. Maybe he knows that down the road a few thousand years people like us will exist—self-proclaimed Jesus lovers who, for whatever reason, glance over the hard portions of Scripture that communicate clearly that one of our roles as disciples is to love and serve the poor.

Do not merely listen to the word, and so deceive yourselves. Do what it says. Anyone who listens to the word but does not do what it says is like someone who looks at his face in a mirror and, after looking at himself, goes away and immediately forgets what he looks like. But whoever looks intently into the perfect law that gives freedom, and continues in it—not forgetting what they have heard, but doing it—they will be blessed in what they do. (James 1:22–25 NIV)

Why should we look in the mirror? The mirror is how we process who we are, what needs to be done, and whether we are on the right path or drifting from living out God's will.

So the question we must ask is this: When I look into the mirror, what do I see? When I was in Zimbabwe I was forced to look into the mirror of real life, and I hated the reflection—a missional church planter who ignored the global orphan crisis. I did not offer my fellow international pastors a hand in friendship. Instead I stayed in my *comfort* zone while these pastors lived in a *war* zone and dealt with issues too big for them to fight alone. Those issues require the *whole* body of Christ.

I realized that I left Pastor John alone to fight for the gospel on his own. I represented the wealthiest Christians in the world while Pastor John represented the poorest Christians. I quickly learned that we have so much to offer each other. Our callings are different, but they point us toward the same place.

Pastor John's church members have faith that is simple and fantastic. I learned more about faith in Zimbabwe than all my years in Bible college. They have a joy that is out of this world, while my joy is based on the stuff of this world. I realized that I had access to resources the church in Zimbabwe could not even dream about, yet I kept those resources to myself. Apparently I forgot that I belong to a *global* Church.

When I looked in the mirror, I saw something horrible and beautiful. I realized that sometimes we have to do the hard things before we get to the good things. God loves you and me too much to allow us to ignore Scripture.

God knows something you and I don't know—his way is far better than our way! As a disciple of Jesus, it took me years to fully realize this idea. God simply had a better way for me to live. I was so busy building my dreams that I ignored the dreams God had for me. His way is filled with beauty and meaning and hope.

No doubt we have to slow down, look in the mirror, and deal with reality, which for you might be that your life is not aligned with the life God has called you to live. Maybe you recognize yourself in how I felt: my life was consumed by pursuing my version of the American dream, creating a culture of safety, a place where I did not have to trust God for anything. If this is what you see when you look in the mirror, I have tremendous news for you—grace is alive and well.

He can use me. He can use you. Why? Because he uses ordinary people to do his extraordinary work.

We serve a God who loves us deeply and desires us to live on mission tangibly. If we do not look into the mirror, we may miss an opportunity to partner with God, live a meaningful life, and leave a lasting legacy. When we do look into the mirror, we can pause, talk with God, and ask him to give us wisdom and faith so we can live a life that will glorify his name and serve our broken, global neighbors.

# What Gospel Justice Really Means

When I began to talk about the theology of justice, many of my conservative friends started to question me. They thought I was preaching a social gospel. "What about evangelism and worship?"

The gospel simply means "the good news of Jesus."

Justice simply means "making what is wrong, right."

Gospel justice is the good news of Jesus that makes what is wrong, right.

When a child is hungry, the good news is a plate of food.

When a little girl is trapped in a brothel, being abused and used, the good news is rescue.

When a father is without a job and forced to give up his child to an orphanage, the good news is employment.

When a community is drinking dirty water, the good news is clean water.

When a teenager is homeless, the good news is an invitation to live with a new family and have a place to belong.

When we assume that the gospel is only evangelism, church planting, or worship, we lose our opportunity to show the full love and power of Jesus, who was others-focused and full of compassion and love. Broken communities need to see God's people fully loving them. The Gospels are very clear on this: Jesus focused both on spiritual *and* physical needs.

I was in Haiti walking down a mountainside, talking to a

mission pastor from an American megachurch. We talked about the lack of clean water as he watched men, women, and children walk up and down the mountain to fetch dirty water from the stream.

After watching a young boy carrying a huge, white bucket of water on his head on his way back up the steep mountain, my friend said, "Why does it matter if we bring these people clean water if they don't know the gospel?"

My first thought: I want to punch you in the face.

My second thought: I want to push you down the mountain.

My third thought: I want you to drink dirty water, get really sick, experience diarrhea, miss work, lose your job, have no money to pay for your kids to eat or attend school, and then I want you to drop your child off at a local orphanage so that child can live.

Yes, I'm being dramatic, but my friend's thought is indicative of many church leaders. Their focus on worship and evangelism causes them to miss other opportunities to show God's love by caring for the daily needs of the suffering and by asking their people to engage in simple, powerful deeds of justice.

The prophet Isaiah saw this issue as well, and the first chapter of his book is a powerful reminder of how the church can often frustrate God when we fail to look into the mirror and see what we have become. Isaiah told his people that God was upset because they were failing to care for the poor and God was irritated with their false sense of worship—their worship had become worthless. It had less to do with action, compassion, and service and more to do with attendance and following religious rituals, which is not exactly what God had in mind for his people.

Do you relate to this story? You know God has so much more for you, but you feel stuck in a rut—wanting to break out and experience more of God's kingdom in your life and in your family's life.

You can take small, powerful steps to move toward a life filled with compassion, a life in which God uses your gifts to bring hope to the hurting. Imagine a God who is excited to show up and be with his people because they are not religious. Rather, they are deeply committed to becoming a people who love God, love others, and seek justice. They want to usher in what is right because of the cross and resurrection.

In Isaiah 1 we see a people who couldn't care less about those who are being destroyed by the Enemy. They had no compassion on the poor, they ignored the injustices of the world, and because of that, they offended God.

But, God, who is full of grace and mercy, and who desires to see his people flourish, and live in his will, presented a pathway forward.

God then told them to do this:

Cease to do evil, learn to do good; seek justice, correct oppression, bring justice to the fatherless, plead the widow's cause. (Isaiah 1:16–17 ESV)

Let's process this for a moment. "*Learn to do good*" simply tells us that, if left alone to our own desires, we will not take time to look in the mirror. We will pursue lives that please ourselves rather than seeking the desires of the God we claim to worship.

While this Scripture seems harsh, God is trying to communicate with grace to his children a more meaningful way to live—a more others-focused life—which is worship that truly satisfies God.

*"Seek justice."* Going back to James, it's not enough to know; instead, as Bob Goff would say, "Love Does." Seeking justice proves to the world that you are a doer of God's Word. Imagine that God's people are actively striving to bring evil into the light and seeing wrong made right. This is the meaning of justice. It is the good news; it is what God calls us to participate in as individuals, families, and communities. Yes, you, your family, and friends are called to seek justice together!

*"Correct oppression."* The word "correct" is vital. It means we have to fix something that is wrong. We need to see a manifested transformation. Oppression is a weight that we carry and can't shake or solve. It's frustrating because if we are oppressed, we have an oppressor; we need to be delivered so we can become free. If a community lacks clean water, correcting oppression is to help provide water; if a community is oppressed by violence, we can correct the violence by creating safety and peace. If women are not treated as equals, if they are being oppressed because of their gender, we can stand up with them and for them and make sure they experience the joy of equal rights. Do you get the picture? Does it make sense to you? Normal people like you and me—together with our family, friends, and our church communities—can become committed to seeing oppression crushed by love and grace if we are willing to take action.

*"Bring justice to the fatherless."* Life has gone wrong for the

orphaned. They need redemption; they need food; they need education; and they need a sense of belonging. They need a family who will care for them, keep them safe, show them love, and help them transition to adulthood. If no one intervenes, these kids will have little shot at a real life; their hopes will be dashed by their circumstances, and they will spend their lives trying to survive day by day. They will often end up homeless. They will be trafficked. Many will become hardened criminals and die at a young age—they are the most vulnerable of all.

*"Plead the widow's cause."* A widow in Isaiah's time had no rights and almost no hope. They had to (and, sadly, *still* have to) deal with issues of land rights, being able to work and provide, and not being abused. How can the church be countercultural and defend them, care for them, love them, support them, empower them, and make them feel loved?

Isaiah, just like James, lays out what the good news of justice should look like. Isaiah presents a clear picture and a bold message to God's people. Thankfully he also gives us a clear way forward that simplifies what it means to pursue justice and care for the poor. When we care for the poor, we get the joy of experiencing a God who uses us to do his work on his behalf.

## My Near-Death Experience on the Nile

Sometimes true understanding and empathy requires us to experience something that will help us understand what is at stake.

In 2013 I was in Uganda visiting our staff and our local leader,

Edward. After a week of taxing work, the kind of work that leaves you zapped of all energy, my friend Tim wanted to raft the Nile River. Tourists come from all over the world to experience the mighty Nile and her class 3, 4, 5, and 6 rapids (as a point of reference, you have to walk around the 6s).

The next morning, we were excited to start our journey down the Nile. As we drove to our base camp, I could see the mighty rapids. I was excited and a bit nervous. We slipped on some life jackets, met our guide, Tutu, and pushed the rafts off into the calm Nile. Tutu gave us "safety training" before we started to paddle toward the rapids.

"If you fall out of the boat, just try and hold on to the rope. But, if you can't, don't panic; eventually, the river will spit you out. It always does."

With our "training" over, we started to paddle. I kept just thinking "I'm on *the Nile River* with some of my best friends." Though everything was smooth, I did wonder about that safety "training." Oh well—I was sure we would not need it.

After going through a class 3 and a class 4, I felt like an expert. This was easy-breezy; we were taming this sacred river with each stroke of our oars. Then we arrived at the class 6 rapid. Now, that was intimidating. Thankfully, it is illegal to raft the class 6, so we had to paddle to the shore and carry our raft over a massive rock, down a small dirt pathway, and to the other side of the class 6 rapid. We took a moment and enjoyed the epic sight of the water churning, swirling. Tutu rallied us around him, and he was suddenly very serious. He said, "Friends, we have one more rapid, and then we are done. But, you have three options: Easy, Medium, or Hard."

Easy = you probably will not flip.
Medium = you might flip.
Hard = you most definitely will flip.

Tutu wanted us to decide which part of the class 5 rapid we wanted to go through. The group chose the medium rapids. We were too scared to choose the hard rapids and there was no way we could choose the easy rapids; that decision would irreparably wound our egos.

As in his earlier "training," which was rushed and a bit short on details, Tutu was vague with his communication. He neglected to tell us that we had to go *past* the hard rapid to get to the medium rapid. So we paddled, and suddenly Tutu is screaming like a madman: "*Harder! Harder! Harder!*" Then he says, "We're not going to make it . . . we're not going to make it."

And just like that, the *hard* part of this class 5 rapid consumed us. When the mighty water hit us, it felt like a Mike Tyson uppercut. I was immediately thrown from the raft and found myself flipping and spinning underwater. For the first time in my life I understood how clothes in the washing machine must feel. I was doing everything in my power to break the water's surface, but I was held powerless under the power of the class 5 rapid.

My breath was running out. I had never felt so hopeless and weak in all my life. Was I going to make it?

Finally, Tutu's world-class training came to fruition. The river spit me out roughly one hundred yards downstream. I was discombobulated, out of breath, confused, and worried about the rest of my team. My friend, Tim, was right next to me trying to get me to hold on to his paddle; he finally yelled, "*Grab the paddle!*"

The lifeboat, which was waiting in case anyone flipped out of a raft (like me), came to pick us up. The Australian lifeguard asked, "Hey mate, you okay? Man, that was scary."

## Get in the Boat

Thankfully, we were all fine. I share this story because right now in our world billions of people are feeling the same way I felt under the water. Will anyone come help me? They are being tossed to and fro, and they need everyday people like you and me to get into a lifeboat and help them out of the rapids of poverty and back to a safe spot.

What if doing good was simple? That is the question I wrestle with every day. I can't help but think of God's people—everyday, normal people like you and me—and how he can use us to be people who get in a lifeboat, head out into the dangerous rapids, and help rescue folks being crushed by the evils of this world.

You and I alone cannot be a lifeboat to the 150 million vulnerable kids and orphans, the thirty million slaves, the over four hundred thousand American kids trapped in the foster care system. Our capacity is not that big, nor does God call us to fix the entire world's problems. But he calls us to do something.

We can change the life of one child through sponsorship, help rescue one slave, foster one kid, or feed one homeless person on our street. We can help rescue people from the rapids of suffering and use our resources, talents, and passions to see their lives transformed.

Here's the deal—my story is a bit dramatic and possibly abnormal. Your story is probably different. What I know is this: those people who took me to the camp—those people who invited me to live with them? They were normal. Teachers and plumbers and youth pastors—they were my lifeboat. They rescued me and brought me to a safe place where I could make sense of the world.

They did not sell their homes and move to another country, nor did they start nonprofits. They were just everyday, normal families who were willing to allow God to use them to love a kid in desperate need. And now my organization is doing the same on behalf of orphans around the globe. We have teachers, small business owners, churches, stay-at-home moms, pastors, financial advisers, and others who are all helping bring hope to those living in extreme poverty. They are making an impact in the world. We are all getting in our lifeboats and heading out on the river, ready to help people in need. Will you join us? It will be one of the best decisions of your life!

# Despite Your Fears and Failures

## *Believing You Are Good Enough Because God Is Good*

Do all the good you can.

By all the means you can.

In all the ways you can.

In all the places you can.

At all the times you can.

To all the people you can.

As long as ever you can.

John Wesley

I remember the sleepless nights. My mind would be filled, and it could not stop working. One night I woke up at 2:00 a.m. and started to create our first business plan. The news was on in the background while I wrote down my hopes and dreams. All I could hear was how our economy was facing its worst fall since the Depression in the '30s. I was so scared that if I started something new it would flop. I would be a forty-something guy who had to live with his in-laws and face the fact that not only did I fail in helping those thirty orphans in Zimbabwe, but I had also created another crisis for my family.

Fear gripped me, but the decision was final—I was going to launch a nonprofit. I was praying that it would turn into a movement of normal, everyday people who had a desire to do good and make a difference.

I sat down with my copastor to tell him I was stepping down. God was calling me to seek justice and care for orphans vocationally. We began to create a transition plan for the church for the next year or so. Honestly, I had no clue what I had just done. I had no idea that in the following years the economy would crumble, the housing market would plummet, and life as we know it would change forever.

Over the next year I spent my early mornings and late evenings in research because I had no idea how to launch a nonprofit. Neither my years in ministry nor the corporate world prepared me for this.

However, you impact the world by taking tiny steps in the right direction—a direction that is dedicated to solving problems and making the world better. For me it was starting a new organization; for you it may be rearranging your budget to sponsor a child, giving a $25 microloan to empower an entrepreneur, changing your shopping habits to buy jewelry from an artisans' collective group, or serving one Saturday a month at your local homeless shelter.

I started meeting with many of my pastor friends to seek advice; one such meeting was with Michael "Stew" Stewart. He had just moved to Austin and was on staff at the Austin Stone Community Church.

As we sat in a coffee shop, Stew began to shape much of the direction for the nonprofit. He recommended books like *When Helping Hurts* and *Walking with the Poor*. He also connected me with a CEO of a large nonprofit organization doing the exact type of work that I wanted to accomplish.

A few weeks later I met with this CEO, who offered a piece of life-changing advice: he told me to "break all the rules" and start something that matters. This well-respected leader gave me permission to move forward, to believe that I could do something different and effective, and yet, with this vision, I would not be recreating the wheel. It was the push I needed.

## Putting My Money Where My Mouth Was

In October 2008 I received a call from my copastor, Jeff, who had just received a call from Matt, the pastor of the Austin Stone. The conversation went something like this:

"Hey, Marlow. Matt just called me. He had heard that you wanted to start a nonprofit, so he pitched me this idea: what if our little 100-member church became part of the Austin Stone. I (Jeff) will be able to relieve Matt by speaking more, and our church will become the north campus."

There it was—the moment I knew needed to move forward.

My church that I copastored along with Jeff now had a way forward, something that was very important to me. Forty-five days later we had our final service as Vista Community Church. We prayed, we worshiped, and we said good-bye to the past and hello to the future. And just like that, I was out of a job.

My wife was so happy with me!

## When Everything Goes Wrong

We had built a transition plan, and I had raised money from churches and private donors to launch the nonprofit and provide for my family. But remember, this was November 2008 and the economy was tanking. I had no idea just how bad it was going to be and how long it would last.

I had verbal commitments of close to $100,000, which meant we had six months of financial stability to start the organization, but within one month those commitments dwindled to $1,000—about one week of operating costs. The economy was falling faster than a falling star, and financial apocalypse seemed certain.

ONE THOUSAND DOLLARS.

ONE WEEK.

I panicked as confidence in my plan and God shrank. How was I going to help these kids in Zimbabwe? How was I going to pay my own bills? How was I going to afford my coffee and breakfast taco habits? (Trust me—this is essential to living in Austin.) I reminded myself that God is good, and he wants to use normal people like me to do good. His ways are not common, even though he uses common people. No matter what the stock market suggested, God had a plan, and I needed to take a small step forward, again and again.

I had some friends, good friends, who worried for me. They gave me advice like, *"Go get a real job!"* and asked questions like, *"Why haven't you gone to get a job yet?"* A few friends from local churches even reached out to offer me a staff position. Everyone was just trying to survive, hoping that the next round of layoffs would not include them!

Many of my pastor friends saw their budgets decrease significantly. It was next to impossible to commit to a new partnership when they were just trying to sustain the church and their current partners.

Remember, I was the kid who grew up in a trailer park. I can still remember standing in the welfare line every week with my mother to collect our cheese, bread, and milk. We struggled to make ends meet. Now I was in my mid-thirties with a wife and two kids, and I had no plan B! I was so scared that I would have to stand in that welfare line again, this time as a husband, father, and failed minister.

I was getting angry. How could these people and those churches renege on their commitments? How could God thrust me into this journey if it was a dead end? Why was the economy falling apart so rapidly and with no end in sight? The timing could not be worse. I remember lying awake at night, begging God not to let me fail.

Have you been there and experienced those moments, when you're trying desperately to hold on to faith, but all you really want to do is curl up like a baby and cry?

A lemonade stand was one thing, but now it was all or nothing. The kids in Zimbabwe needed help, and the kids in my own home needed provision as well.

When you make an intentional decision to do good, when you start taking small steps forward, you will have crossroads experiences. You will reach a place where you can turn back to safety or turn toward the hard direction of your dreams. Will you push through when failure seems imminent, or will you return to ease and comfort?

I was constantly second-guessing myself. Was I good enough? Did I have enough faith? Was God for this? Could I stay focused and try to move forward one day at a time?

This is usually the part in the story that there is a massive midnight breakthrough, where God audibly answers prayers—and then the next day an anonymous check arrives for one million dollars.

Right?

But here's the truth. God did not speak to me (audibly), we had no money, all my friends thought I was totally insane, and my dog would no longer sit next to me because we had to cut out the dog treats from the budget.

It's in these moments when you really decide what life is all about and where to put your effort and energy. I kept looking in the mirror, remembering those kids in Zimbabwe, reading Scripture, and trying so hard to believe.

I questioned myself. "Who am I to start a nonprofit? Who am I to understand global poverty issues? Who am I to ask people to donate money in the midst of the current economic collapse?" I'm just a normal guy living a normal life.

The enemy will always use fear, doubt, guilt, and condemnation to hold us back from pursuing our dreams and making an impact.

*What if we fail?*

*What if the critics are right?*

*What if we run out of money?*

Brennan Manning recounts this story about Mother Teresa. She was asked to pray that a coworker would receive clarity for his next steps in life. She laughed and refused, saying, *"I have never had clarity; what I have always had is trust. So I will pray that you trust God."*[1]

I began to ask the questions, "What if God was in this? If so, is he not bigger than my fears? Is he concerned with the current state of the economy?" I realized that God did not say to care for orphans only when it is easy.

What if God wanted me to fight for this dream, take one step forward every day, and trust him? After all, is this not what Pastor John taught me in Zimbabwe? What if God wanted me (or what if God wants you) to believe that he is bigger than my fears, doubts, and concerns?

God tells us in Matthew 6:26 that he cares for the birds. Then he asks us a question: are we not more valuable than birds?

You are not good enough because you are good; *you are good enough because God is good.* He is a God who uses normal people who have messed up, screwed up, failed many times over—people who don't have it all together, but they have something far more valuable than being perfect: they have passion and willingness to allow God to use them to change the world.

You are good enough to be a world changer. You can change the world of one person or an entire community or country.

I slowly began to understand this—God wanted to use me, yet he did not want me to carry the entire weight of the world's problems. I'm good enough because God is going to carry the load and take on the real pressure. I just need to be willing to be used by him along the way! I need to stare fear in the face and put my trust in God and his power and love!

It took me a while to realize the valuable lesson God was trying to teach me. I still struggle with the proper words to communicate the depth of the lesson. On many levels, God was crushing my soul, pouring out his heart into my heart.

He loves these kids in Zimbabwe far more than I do. He also loves my daughters far more than I do. He wants to share his burdens with his people. He gave us gifts to be used to make a difference. Yet he also made it very clear that his burden is light and his yoke is easy.

I've had to learn over and over that I cannot solve all the world's problems. God has given a mission to you and me, but he is in full control and we can lean into this truth—God is leading, we are following, and we have to learn how to rely on him.

If we fail to do this, good people who care about others deeply but try to serve out of their own strength will get frustrated and walk away when they realize that they do not possess the power to make the changes they want to see. Only God does!

This subtle but vital truth will empower us to know that we are good enough, we are gifted, we share the burden with Christ, and yet we don't have to carry the impossible weight of fixing all the world's problems. This means we are free to serve, love, fight for good, and yet we can rest our souls because God is in full control.

## Journey through Scripture

God has a funny way of accomplishing his goals. He tends to take the foolish things of the world and use them in silly ways. This will never make sense to most people—I mean, how can it? It's crazy talk.

In Scripture God used a prostitute to rescue spies, a teenager to interpret the dreams of a ruthless king, a shepherd boy to fight a giant, humble fishermen to be the first disciples, and a brutal mercenary who persecuted and killed Christians to go to the Gentiles and share the good news, plant churches, care for the poor, and pen a large portion of the New Testament.

Actually, let's stop here for a moment to see how this all unfolded in the first century. Remember, these words are our roots—the foundation in which we live out our faith.

Galatians 2 describes a power meeting between the church pillars (leaders). It's an epic encounter—definitely one for the ages—starring:

Paul, the Apostle
Peter, the Rock
James, the half brother of Jesus
John, the Beloved

Titus and Barnabas are hanging around as well; their time is about to come. Paul's writings to Titus are soon to be included in the holy canon!

Paul journeys to Jerusalem. He is no longer the one who threatens Christians; he is now the one who leads them in The Way. He requests a meeting with the church pillars that goes something like this:

Paul: "Gentlemen—I've now been serving for fourteen years and I feel like God is calling me to be a missionary and go to the nations—places like Corinth, Galatia, and Rome—to plant churches. These folks have not ever heard the gospel before. Can I go?"

Peter, John, and James: "Take your boys and do good work. God is with you; you have our blessings.

"Only, we ask one thing: Remember the poor."

Paul responds, almost offended. "Guys! That is the very thing I was eager to do!"

*"Remember the poor!"*

*"That was the very thing I was eager to do!"*

Do you see what I mean? It is easy to miss—skim over—that last command given to Paul: "Remember the poor." Paul, the persecutor of Christians who was educated among society's elite, did not just want to help the poor, but he was eager to do it. No doubt, this is proof that God is creating an upside-down kingdom where the poor and the rich love one another, learn from one another, and give dignity to each other.

Was I eager to serve the poor? The question stung! To me, serving the poor was always a project; it was usually a hassle for most of my Christian life. I did it to check off a box. God is not really into that kind of service.

My faith began to build and my fears began to fade, little by little. I begin to see mini-breakthroughs. I was so eager to serve my friends in Zimbabwe, and I was starting to find hope that we were going to be able to do that.

With much hard work and many prayers, God began to open up doors and provide the funds we needed to launch. We had a dozen or so families commit to monthly support, we had a few generous donors help us with our 501(c)(3) status, and some churches told us they were on board and prepared to help.

I met with anyone and everyone who would give me even a few minutes, and I can still remember the first time a stranger said yes. I called a friend of a friend in Houston. After the meeting was over and I had hung up the phone, I wondered how it went; the man didn't say whether or not he was going to give. A few weeks later, a check came in the mail. I was ecstatic. Every few weeks after, another check arrived. Little by little, we were making progress. I continued to share my story and ask people to help.

In those meetings I realized something that shaped the vision of the organization. Most of my friends wanted to help; they just did not really know how. All they needed was a guide—someone to show them how to help, to give them tools they needed to help, and then to walk alongside them to make sure they did not get overwhelmed and burned out.

## We All Need Guides

I've learned that we all need guides in different areas of life. We need teachers, coaches, and consultants. This is why we read blogs and consume media. This is why we attend church and small groups.

My first guides were Steven and Amy, my friends who moved to Cape Town, South Africa. They invited me to come learn what they were doing. Without their push, I would not have been in Zimbabwe to have that life-altering experience at the gas station.

I realized that my friends back in Austin needed a guide as well. They were very busy with life as usual—school, marriage, family, church, chores, sports. These are the everyday realities we all have to work through. They are very spiritual and also can be very mundane, yet they're still important.

Often I feel frustrated. I see good people trying to live a good life, but they feel trapped and can't fully embrace the goodness of life because of the guilt that has been dumped on them. Many of my friends were ready to help. They did not need guilt or condemnation to motivate them; they needed a glimpse into the lives of the suffering and a guide to show them how to make a difference and still enjoy the good gifts God gave them.

And maybe more importantly, they needed to know that God wanted to partner with them; after all, God is our ultimate guide!

I hope that, in some small way, I can be a guide for you—a guide to encourage you to do good and do it well and an inspiration to care for your neighbor and unleash love in our world. When you go to bed tonight, I want you to close your eyes and dream of a better world, not feel weighed down with guilt or shame. I hope you are excited that God is prepared to use you to help other people also live a good life.

## The Day the World Changed

January 12, 2010, was a normal day for most of the world. The scramble to check off those to-do boxes, hit the gym, get the kids to school, and go to that meeting was most likely in full force. If you lived in Haiti, I'm sure the day started like that as well, but soon the earth would begin to groan and crack. In less than one minute, everything changed for Haitians everywhere.

I often try to understand this life-changing moment. Imagine, one second a mother was feeding her child; the next she was trapped under concrete layers of rubble. One second students were in university learning; the next they were crushed by the building in which they were so proud to be (since so few have access to university in Haiti).

On our first trip to Haiti, one woman told me her story of that fateful day. Like you and me, that day started with all the hustle and bustle of a workday. When work was finished, she took a tap-tap (taxi) home.

She would always take a shower before her kids returned from school and then prepare dinner for her family. This was her daily rhythm, which was why she was in the shower when the earth shook. Her house collapsed, and she was buried under rubble, trapped, unable to move. Tears streamed down her cheeks as she told me that everything was pitch black. She feared that Jesus had come back and she was in hell. I asked her, "Why?" She told me she could not move, it was dark, and all she could hear were the screams of the suffering everywhere!

To this day I still cannot comprehend that. I do not have the words to describe the look in her eyes as she shared her story.

## What If Doing Good Was Simple?

Social media blew up quickly; the images coming out of Haiti were haunting. It did not take long to realize this earthquake was going to be bad—really, really bad.

My heart broke for the Haitian people. I wanted to do something, but our organization was still in its infancy. We hardly even had enough funds to buy stamps. So we decided to get creative. I asked my friends Scotty, Ryan, and Holly if they would be willing to design a shirt we could sell online and donate to key organizations that were doing great work in Haiti and would need more support in this crisis.

Two weeks later we began to sell T-shirts online. We hoped

to sell one or two hundred; instead, we sold over two thousand shirts in a few months. God took our simple idea and helped us send over $24,000 to those ministries in Haiti.

Did you notice the simple steps that led to this gift? Graphic designers used their talent, and because of them we were able to raise capital and support great organizations that were doing vital work on the ground in Haiti. Real lives were impacted, and the leaders of these organizations were encouraged.

And what might be more important to folks like my designer friends—or really anyone—is the joy we find when we realize God's deep desire to partner with everyday, normal people using their talents to do good.

## When Home Is More Like Hell

Occasionally in life, reality hits you hard, and it's so difficult to process. The earthquake in Haiti was massive, and it took its toll on the Haitian people. I knew I could not fix every problem. I could not raise enough money, I could not send enough people, and I was not in a place where I knew exactly the best way to help.

On my second trip to Haiti, my friend Erin, who lived in Haiti working for another organization, asked me if I wanted to visit Pastor St Cyr (pronounced "sincere," which I would come to learn was very apt). He had become famous for serving the people in Tent City—the same Tent City with which actor Sean Penn was involved. Sean and Pastor St Cyr partnered together for a season to serve the people of Haiti who lost their homes, their sense of community, loved ones, jobs, and so much more. All these people had was a tent; they were desperately trying to get back on their feet and make sense of their new normal.

Pastor St Cyr started a church in Tent City to encourage the people and to help with their suffering. Over sixty thousand people lived in this makeshift city on the grounds of a former golf course, and life was a living hell for the folks who called it home.

I remember walking through the tents. The tension was so thick, and I barely saw any life when I looked in the people's eyes. I knew they had been through so much, and their government had few ways to aid them—this was an emergency and they needed help. Pastor St Cyr held church every day, sometime twice a day. Hundreds would come out and worship God together.

They would weep, pray, and with hands raised they would worship. A bunch of kids surrounded me the first night I joined these amazing people. They grabbed my hands and held tightly. We could not speak the same language, so they would open their mouths as if to say, "I'm hungry . . . can you help?"

Some would just sit in my lap, and others would lay their heads on my shoulder.

They just needed to know that hope was available.

They just needed to know that everything was going to be all right.

*They just needed to know that love still existed.*

All I could do was cry, because if I was truthful, I was very angry at God. The suffering was heavy, almost suffocating. As I sat there with these kids, I saw a lady with crutches walking from her tent. She had lost her leg in the earthquake, but soon I would learn she did not lose her faith. She would be another guide and give me the faith that I needed to help her people.

The one-legged warrior walked to the front of the church, grabbed the microphone, and began to share her story. She ended with a simple statement: "I have lost my leg and my home and many people from my family. But I have not lost my faith; so don't have pity on me. Today I'm thankful to be alive and I'm thankful that God is with me."

In that moment she wasn't a victim; she wasn't a poor woman living in a tent. She was a guide, a teacher, a prophetess. Because God works through unlikely people to do incredible things. God used this woman to silence my excuses. She lived with courage; I couldn't help but try to do the same.

## A Whistle Can Change a Life

We sat down with Pastor St Cyr and asked how we could help. He told us that many of the women in the camp were unsafe. They were being assaulted—raped—in the middle of the night because they lacked the protection of a house and a local police force. How could we solve this problem? Someone asked us to bring whistles and pass them out to those women on our next trip to Haiti. I knew I was coming back in a few weeks.

Some friends in Arkansas who were coming to Haiti to do medical work tackled this issue. Stay-at-home moms, doctors, pastors, dentists, and college students each donated a few dollars to purchase bags and bags of whistles. As we went to the church in Tent City, I preached a word of encouragement, and at the end Pastor St Cyr shared about the problem. Most of the ladies were too ashamed to say whether they had been abused, so Pastor told all the women to come up to the front, pick up a whistle, and put it around their necks.

Little by little, they all walked to the front, grabbed a whistle, and returned to their seats. The pastor asked them all to hold their whistles, and together they were going to use them. Just like that, you could hear the shrill sounds streaming through the air.

It was a symphony of hope, of dignity being restored.

Pastor St Cyr said, "If anyone is hurting you at any time, you blow that whistle and we will come to you and help." Soon tears streamed down the cheeks of many of the women in attendance. Others were shy and embarrassed. As I stood up front with Pastor St Cyr as he prayed and closed the service, many of the ladies came up to our team, hugged us, and said, *"Merci."* It was a humbling experience. By no means did we solve all the problems, but that night hundreds of ladies walked out with a one-dollar whistle and *hope*—hope that if they needed help, help would come. This hope was accomplished because God used a few normal people in Arkansas who wanted to do good and make a difference—*and they did!*

Women should never be abused. They should never live in fear, and if someone is abusing them, we need to fix that. This is a justice issue, and that night, as darkness took over the light, as the sounds of worship stopped and the women of this tent city headed back to their makeshift homes, they knew they had help and people cared about their safety.

We cannot fix everything overnight, but we have to start somewhere. That night, we started with a little bit of compassion, a prayer, and a whistle.

We can all make a difference. Sometimes it's big; sometimes it is small. Either way, each act of compassion matters to those who are suffering. Either way, we are "good enough" to make a difference because God is good.

—— 4 ——

# You've Got the Goods

## *The Incredible Truth That You Are Already Equipped*

The good you do today, people will often forget
tomorrow; do good anyway. Give the world the
best you have, and it may never be enough; give
the world the best you've got anyway. You see,
in the final analysis, it is between you and your
God; it was never between you and them anyway.

**Mother Teresa**

My friend Danielle is a teacher in Texas. She met some local teachers while on a trip to Haiti with us, and she wanted to help these teachers teach well. She heard about our Help One Classroom campaign, which raises money specifically to support a classroom. It means teachers can have a fair, living wage (often teachers are not paid in developing countries), purchase school supplies, and get adequate training. Danielle decided to take the summer to raise enough money to support one classroom.

She sold T-shirts and then hosted a party. I remember the

moment she reached her goal and fully funded the classroom. She was ecstatic, and her friends at the party were able to celebrate with her.

I think we all want to do good, do it well, and do it together, and Danielle is a perfect example of why I believe that doing good can be simple yet powerful. Sometimes God just calls us to throw a party so we can make an impact. Now a teacher in Haiti will be able to provide for her family while she follows her calling to teach her students.

Did you know that you are already equipped to do good and do it well? So many people just can't fully embrace this truth. I often tell people that God wants to use them and has already gifted them, and often they respond with disbelief. This makes me frustrated. Why? If you don't feel confident that your life matters, that you can make a difference, that you already have the tools you need, that God is excited to partner with you, you will not allow him to use you. That is a tragedy that could profoundly impact society.

On a recent trip to Texas, I stopped at BREWED in Fort Worth. I couldn't help but notice a tattoo on the barista's arm: "Lord, I believe. Help my unbelief."

Many times I've looked into that aunting mirror and have seen myself—a very broken person—and I've wondered if I'm good enough. I wonder if my life has meaning. I wonder if we're making a difference in the world. I wonder if any of this "doing good" stuff matters. In these moments, if I'm going to continue to fight injustice, I must sa, "Lord, I believe; help my unbelief."

Do you relate? Have you ever looked into the mirror and asked yourself why you exist? What is the purpose of your life? Why do you have certain passions and gifts? If you believe God created you and that God gifted you in a certain way, and if in fact God cares deeply for the poor and wants to partner with his creation to serve and care for the poor, then yes, God wants to partner with you!

Do you struggle to find a sense of peace—that you are in fact a person God wants to use and you have the goods to be used?

Jesus gave each of us gifts, passions, and talents. We use these tools to make a living and pay the bills. Often we do not realize that God gifted these tools for another great purpose—to care for the poor.

I want you to take a moment and wrestle with this, because if you don't believe you can make a difference, you won't attempt to make a difference. It will not be because you don't want to; it will be because you doubt that you can. This doubt will fester and create apathy. An apathetic Christian is a deathblow to those who are suffering, who need someone to hold out an oar and pull them to safety when it seems as if the rapids of life are going to pull them under. And then not only can we pull someone to safety, but we can also empower them to live life well.

## Leave a Mark with Your One Life

I was able to learn firsthand what it meant to leverage what you love and what you're good at, to leave a mark in this world, when in 2012 Help One Now rallied a group of bloggers to take a trip to Haiti: Jen Hatmaker, Sarah Bessey, Deidra Riggs, Jennie Allen, Mary DeMuth, Kristen Howerton, Dan King, and Marty Duane. These are gifted writers who have become experts at their craft. They also have tribes of people who love and respect them. Of course they have a passion to use their gifts to move the hearts of their readers to get involved in issues of justice!

The trip was going really well—until it imploded without warning. We planned to head out into the Haitian countryside, which was about four hours away. Our team needed to come back to the city that same evening since we were flying home the next morning.

As we drove down the beautiful lush mountains of Haiti, we approached the all-too-familiar chaos of Port-au-Prince. Traffic had come to a standstill and we began to worry about our time. We picked up Pastor Gaetan, one of our local Haitian leaders, so he could spend the day with us. We were finally making our way out of the city, already feeling behind, when one of our vehicles broke down.

Some people would say that I'm a paranoid traveler who is dead set on making sure the schedule goes as planned (those people might be right). As soon as the van broke down, everyone looked at me, assuming I was going to melt down. But of course I was supercool under pressure; no Marlow meltdowns in Haiti! We realized that we needed to make new plans since we no longer had time to drive out to the countryside and return. This was our most important day on this trip, and in that moment, it was ruined—so I thought.

# When Dreams Come True

Now, a few years earlier Pastor Gaetan dreamed of building a school for the kids in his community. The earthquake destroyed most of the community schools, so many of the children had nowhere to attend. Help One Now was not ready to build a school yet, so Pastor Gaetan built a tent school. I remember showing up one day and seeing hundreds of kids attending school . . . under tarps supported by wooden sticks. Pastor Gaetan has the biggest smile in Haiti, and that day it was bigger than ever. I hugged him and shed a tear. He is an amazing leader, and he knew how vital it was for kids to return to school.

Two hours later our blogger team was stuck with nothing to do, so we made our way back to Pastor Gaetan's home. On the drive over we talked about how to redeem this day. We only had a few hours, but we had two amazing visual artists (Scotty, a photographer, and Kris, a filmmaker), and we had a van full of storytellers. In the back of the van, I asked Pastor Gaetan if he still wanted to build that school. He nodded his head, smiled, and said, "Of course."

We headed back to Pastor Gaetan's place and began to dream. What if we told a story, and over the holidays each blogger asked their tribe to donate something simple, like a brick. Then, brick by brick, $25 at a time, could we build a school? After ten minutes we were all ready to move forward. Our board chair, Mike Rusch; Lamar Stockton, our Haiti Operations Director; and I sat down with Gaetan to calculate the finances; the bloggers gathered around a table to process how to tell the story; and Scotty and Kris began to dream how they could use film and photography.

Eight hours later we nailed it. The stories were told, videos were recorded, business plans were in place, and prayers were prayed. It was as if God knew all along that this was going to happen!

A month later we went live with the Legacy Project 2012. Thousands of people all over the world began to buy one virtual brick for $25, while some donated far more. Soon we had enough funds to build that school.

For almost three years, about 150 Haitian kids attended school under a tent. That would change on October 2, 2013. That day more than three hundred Haitian kids woke up and trundled off to Williamson Adrien Academy, named in honor of Pastor Gaetan's brother, a victim of the earthquake.

Imagine if these writers went to Haiti and painted an orphanage or hauled some bricks or did some construction project. No doubt it would have felt good for them, but I do not think they would have made the same impact. They had their own unique gifts—their abilities as writers and their tribes that they had built—and they used those gifts to do good and do it well.

You don't have to be a writer with a platform to make a difference. You need a willing heart and a clear understanding of why you exist and how you can help in big and small ways; you already have the gifts, now you just have to use them!

One of my greatest fears, and what might be one of the greatest obstacles to ending or putting a massive dent in extreme poverty alleviation, is this: when everyday, normal people feel as if they can't help. Let me repeat: this is a tragedy.

*In fact, I would say it is the ordinary people who will determine how much impact is done in the world.* It's the ordinary folks who have a great responsibility. If individuals like you and me decide in our hearts to be deliberate and care for the poor, there is no doubt we can truly see the majority of extreme poverty vanish into thin air. We're already making tremendous progress!

Scripture gives us a model that makes sense to me. Ephesians 4:9–16 gives us a glimpse into some ecclesiology, which is a fancy word that really means biblical structure or how the church is designed to work.

Jesus is the head. The King. The Messiah. The Teacher.

You and me—we're the students, the disciples. Jesus is the star; we are the servants. We are created in the image of God. We all have a purpose in life to follow in the footsteps of Jesus. We are all called and equipped to do good works that prove we are disciples of Jesus—not people of religion—by the fruit that we produce. We are not called to do this alone; again, we are disciples, and we are in this together. We are family and we have a mission, and we each have key roles.

This will never fully make sense, yet it totally does. We do not deserve any of this. It is hard to put into words what this means—the depth, the meaning, the purpose, and the opportunity.

We have to fully capture this essence and let it sink in: Jesus is calling you to partner with him—*you, the imperfect, the broken, the sinful, the overwhelmed, the confused.* It's crazy . . . but it's *true*. His grace is amazing, his love is deep, and his power is present and ready to transform you and use you to help transform others!

You are a disciple of Jesus; he is teaching us—his people—how to live life well. Jesus asks his people to live differently and to use our gifts to make a difference. Our Teacher tells us that one day all of this pain and brokenness will end. The tears of the broken will no longer be shed; the pain will be gone. Justice will flow like a river, and all the wrongs will be made right.

But for now, we live in the in-between moments. Yes, Jesus is resurrected—the final outcome is no longer in question. But the journey is not over; a battle of good and evil rages on and on and on. It is real, it is thick, it is horrible, and the Devil is seeking to devour while he still has time.

And who stands in the way of this evil enemy?

The church.

Who is the church?

*You are the church.*

## When the Church Is on the Move

According to Matthew 5:16, the church is filled with disciples who are called and equipped to glorify God through their good works. These works prove that Jesus is alive in us. Jesus gave us tools to leverage along the way, and then he sent the Holy Spirit to lead and empower us. The Holy Spirit carries the burden that we can't bear. Each day we cast our cares on him!

Let's dig a little deeper; this is important, soul-shifting truth. If you get this, you will never be the same!

When a group of people from Arkansas purchases a bag of whistles, when a teacher from Austin throws a party and sponsors a classroom, when a stranger from Houston is generous and gives to help launch an organization, when a group of writers help fund a school—these are small examples of what it means to live out the good news. They weren't making dramatic lifestyle changes. They weren't picking up and moving overseas. They used their gifts—the very things that make them who they are—to do simple acts of good. *Significant* acts of good.

We were never called just to be a people who believe in certain theological outcomes and attend worship gatherings that teach us more and more about Jesus. Rather, we were called to live out our faith in the highways and byways of society, where love seeps into the hardness of hearts and melts away suffering, pain, and heartbreak—where good overcomes evil and love conquers all.

Christianity cannot be known for pew sitters, angry preachers, judgmental Christians, and graceless communities. Rather, we must be known as a people who show God's goodness by doing good.

# You Are Called and Gifted to Solve Problems

From him the whole body, joined and held together by every supporting ligament, grows and builds itself up in love, as each part does its work.

*Ephesians 4:16*

Jesus is the head. He has called some to be experts, to help solve these problems as a vocation so that the everyday kingdom-minded doers can be equipped. These are the people who create change; these people are the heart and soul of society, the glue that makes it stick.

I cannot create change as a CEO of a development organization. I can help lead change, I can inspire change, I can create pathways for change, I can empower people to create change, but I have limits. I can't go where you can go; I don't have the gifts, resources, and capacity you have.

The hope is to be a church on the move, each member of the body focused on doing good by using their talents, doing it well by offering dignity, and doing it together in community. No doubt, we have a desire to live a meaningful life, to be used by God to solve real problems, and to help real people in the process. When you love the least of these, you will unlock another layer of meaning in your life.

Then those who are helping and those who are being helped each realize that God is orchestrating a beautiful story.

# When God's People Make God Angry

I know what you are thinking: "How can I make a difference?" Here's the deal. We grow up in a culture that tends to tell us that we need to follow a particular pathway to success. We work hard to provide a good life for our families, and that's a good thing; that's the American dream.

It's easy to cloak ourselves in individualism or even create a life focused on just our own families. Prioritizing our families is absolutely essential, but mission goes far beyond our families and must land in the backyards and front porches of our neighbors—neighbors who could be across the street or across the ocean.

I don't want my primary mission in life to be building the Marlow Family Empire. If we come to the end of life and all we did was serve our families and not our neighbors, did we really fulfill our call? I want my family to be others-focused first, and to build God's kingdom. We have gifts, talents, and passions, but if we choose to view those gifts as ways to build only our own kingdoms, we miss out on the most wonderful gifts in the world—partnering with God to love our neighbors.

What is the worst news ever for God? I think it would be for us to live our lives for ourselves. That breaks God's heart, for his people, who have been forgiven, embraced his grace, and experienced his love shouldn't be capable of ignoring the needs of others. Maybe this is why God was so frustrated in Isaiah. Read Isaiah 1:1–16 to try and get a sense of God's frustration. He knew his people had drifted from what he called them to do.

The spouse, the house, the cars, the savings accounts, the vacations, the white picket fence, the high-rise condo downtown . . . none of these are bad when we have our priorities straight. Truthfully, all of these things can be good gifts from God. We go wrong when our life's pursuit is obtaining those items, when they become idols and get in the way of our calling.

And truthfully, if we are honest with ourselves, we all have this deep, mundane existence that drives us crazy. We know we were created for more, but we're on a treadmill—life—and we can't seem to stop it; it can be maddening!

Why is that? Because sometimes we drift (at least, I do). And when we drift, God's design breaks down. We stop growing, love is shoved to the side, apathy takes over, and guess what? The world suffers the consequence of God's people who resemble the image of the world more than the image of God!

Do you remember the biblical story of Ananias and Sapphira? This story is really scary. The church has just started, and Jesus' people finally "get it." Jesus is resurrected and the Holy Spirit has come. The first four chapters of Acts are a thrilling experience of epic proportions.

Then it all comes to a grinding halt because two people decided to build their own kingdom instead of God's kingdom. They never fully bought in; they never embraced the way of Jesus; they never truly became disciples. Apparently they thought they could live a better life. They became liars.

And it cost them everything.

I don't want to do that. I don't want to be like that. Yet I know I sometimes lie to myself and try to create better outcomes. Like Ananias and Sapphira, I look for the path of least resistance, the path that will fuel my flesh but leave my soul bone dry and my spirit far from God.

What if doing good was simple? I fully believe it is. But simple does not mean easy. Sometimes doing good requires much from us. Because, ultimately, Jesus desires you and me to follow him, embrace his ways, and mature in the faith.

I'm not sure about you, but I think it is time for change anyway. I think it is time we stop allowing the pressures of culture to dictate how we live. We have a King who sent his Son, who chose to show us a better way.

We must realize that the way Jesus teaches his people to live is radically different from how the world teaches us to live. The world will tell you that your money is yours and to do whatever you want with it—whatever makes you happy, it's your life.

Jesus tells us that nothing is ours; it's all his. We get to steward money in a way that honors God and is used for his kingdom. For a disciple, this is beautiful because we desire nothing more than for Jesus to use our money to advance the kingdom. This is why Paul was *eager* to serve the poor.

The world will tell you to use your gifts to build your empire, to platform your name, and to pursue your dreams. You have one life; live it up, party hard, consume more.

Jesus tells us to focus less on ourselves and more on others, to use our gifts to serve people, the rich and the poor. Heck . . . Jesus goes so far as to say that we have to forgive those who hurt us and to love our enemies.

This way of thinking is only radical outside the confines of the gospel. To those who have experienced the love and beauty of Jesus, this is ordinary.

Yes or no—are you ready for the better way? Change always begins with intentional choices. And once you decide, you can embrace the calling to do good and solve problems that will improve the world.

## Ordinary Good

I have the privilege of leading trips. These are not traditional short-term missions; we prefer to call them "pilgrimages." On a mission trip, you tend to want to accomplish something short-term, like a project. This can be good or bad.

We feel that there is a better story, a story that starts with a journey to learn about God, ourselves, and the community needs. We throw down the paintbrushes, drop the bricks, shut down the cameras.

We slow down and listen. Usually our hearts begin to break, one story at a time. Because we prioritize listening over doing, we build a deep bond—a bond that lasts.

After we listen, we begin to dream. How can God use us, the ordinary, to truly see this community transformed? What role can I play? How can I use my gifts to help?

This is what good news looks like in the flesh. God uses everyday, normal, redeemed people to create a better world. This calling has no borders; it extends into all of humanity. These people usually do not have PhDs in Community Development, and no one would consider them experts in global affairs.

They are people who choose to use their gifts to change the world. They are thoughtful, focused, and prepared to learn. They struggle to find a balance in life, as we all do. But they've also learned that they can lean into God's calling, use their gifts to make the world better, and still have an amazing life.

## My Favorite Dentist

Dentists scare me. I avoid them at all cost. I think I would prefer stepping on a colony of fire ants to being in a dentist's chair. The pokes of the needle and sounds of that awful drill? I have a true phobia of dentists.

But I do have a favorite dentist—Don. He is a successful dentist in his sixties, and he is calm, gentle, and enthusiastic. He owns his practice, has raised a beautiful family, and enjoys a wonderful life. Don started to attend Austin New Church and heard about a pilgrimage trip they were taking to Haiti with Help One Now.

This piqued Don's interest, so he signed up. Don's life was radically changed on that trip. He spent a few days doing some simple dentistry work for some of the orphans we care for in Haiti. By the end of the trip, Don knew God had gifted him not only to use dentistry to make a living and help people in Austin but also to use that gift to help people in Haiti and all over the world.

Today Don is doing just that. In the year after he returned from Haiti, he started to research how he could help long term. He met with the dean of a Haitian dentistry school and began to build a relationship. Eventually Don partnered with another organization (after all, there is no need to recreate the wheel), and they now help empower Haitian dentists. They have raised money to help rebuild a dentistry school and to buy new equipment and technology. The goal is to help Haitian dentists do the actual work and to create jobs for them.

Don often travels to Haiti, and he loves it. He would say that his life is more fulfilled now than ever. He is using his gifts in practical ways to make a big impact in the world, and yet he is still very much the same person. Don is making an impact because he is building relationships and processing how to make a real difference. He did not go for seven days, do some mission work, and then disappear back to his life.

Don is creating a better future for Haitians. We spent hours together processing how to do good and do it well, asking, "How do we really help and not hurt?" Don did not run off and try to change the world on his own; rather, he took time to listen to those who are vocationally called to do this work. Together we were able to help Don get started and do work that matters— work that will bring dignity and change to Haiti.

Don still lives in the same house, still runs his practice, and still enjoys the fruit of his labors. His life is completely changed in so many ways, but not in that radical sort of way you may assume.

## Ordinary = The New Radical

Maybe ordinary is the new radical. We go about our days helping to make the world better, just like Don.

He did not move to Haiti, nor did he sell his house or business. Instead he created a plan and used his gifts. This is what we mean when we answer, "It is" to the question "What if doing good was simple?"

Katie is a teacher who took a pilgrimage trip to Haiti with her church. Her life was impacted, and she shared her stories with her husband, Joe, when she returned home. Joe runs a finance firm that helps people grow their wealth and manage their money.

We were discussing our previous trips to Haiti with friends over dinner one night. I got to meet Joe and catch up with Katie. Joe wanted to learn more, so he asked to go on an upcoming pilgrimage to Zimbabwe and Uganda. Ninety days later we were on a plane together.

Joe and Katie are ordinary people. They live in a nice, family neighborhood, work hard at their jobs, are successful, and enjoy life—just like Don.

As we walked down the dusty red dirt roads of Uganda and met people who were suffering from extreme poverty, you could see Joe's heart break. He asked questions. "I'm just a finance guy.

How could I help these people?" Maybe you've been there as well. Extreme poverty seems so overwhelming and can be paralyzing. It's terribly frustrating—you want to do good, but how?

I asked Joe simple questions: "How can we help these people live a better life? How can your gifts in finance and business make an impact? How can Katie's gift in child development make an impact?" You see—this is the key question. Joe, Katie, and Don are passionate about specific issues that matter to them. How can we focus that passion to unleash their human capital to do good and love their neighbors around the world?

Don, Joe, and Katie are part of our tribe. We are able to help guide them, and Help One Now could never succeed without them. They're examples of hundreds of people who have realized they are gifted and can use those gifts to make a difference.

Here's how this has worked practically:

1. They have been generous to Help One Now.
2. Joe is on our finance team. He is using his gifts to make us a better organization, which will impact the world.
3. Katie helps lead our education collective. She raises funds throughout the year to help pay salaries for teachers and purchase needed school supplies for classrooms.
4. Don empowers Haitian dentists so they can serve their people.

They're using their gifts to make a difference in the here and now, and we are also positioning them to make a long-term difference through job training, microlending, business development, and teacher training.

Joe can help these folks run a thriving business so they can provide for their family and be generous to their community. Katie can empower teachers with new techniques and data so they are informed and prepared to teach well. And of course Don does the same with Haitian dentists.

## Unleash Human Capital

When most folks think of missions work, they feel they need to write a check or take a short-term trip. Being generous and donating is incredible, and taking a trip can be life changing and helpful, but I think we need to dig deeper. Why? Because God has equipped you for his good work. How do we unleash your human capital for long-term good, not short-term excitement?

That is a question worth pondering! Don, Katie, and Joe are not experts in community development, nor do they have fancy degrees in global affairs. What they do have is passion and expertise and the belief that God has already equipped them to do what he calls them to do. You and I are no different.

# 5

# Not Just Good on Paper

## *Good Is People, Not Projects*

As the Father has sent me, I am sending you.

**Jesus**

On my first trip to Zimbabwe in 2007, we drove from the Johannesburg airport to the border of Zimbabwe. I had no idea that in just a few hours I would meet that boy at the gas station and my life would completely change.

On our way we stopped at a small town in northeast South Africa to meet a pastor named Willie, who happened to give me a camouflage hat.

I still remember that hat.

Willie took us to his village, and I noticed something strange as he showed us around and introduced us to his community. One of the buildings—I think it was an orphanage—had chipped paint. I could see the layers and many colors. I asked Willie why there were so many colors, and he looked at me awkwardly.

Every summer, teenagers from America come visit for a few weeks. They usually play soccer with the kids and do a VBS.

Each year they also paint the orphanage. Willie told me he did not know what to do with these teenagers, and usually it caused a lot of stress on the community.

In Africa, when you are the host, you go all out. It is just the culture. My friend Steven then told me how many students had come the previous summer and what their churches (and parents) had paid for them to visit: close to $100,000. This is a lot of money; if we're going to spend this kind of cash, it's kind of important that we ask what the return on investment is for the kingdom and what the tangible impact on the local community is, right?

Kids in Africa know how to play soccer, the local church knows how to do a Vacation Bible School, and the orphanage does not need a new paint job every summer. Furthermore, if they did, plenty of locals know how to paint. There's a good chance—in fact, it is nearly a certainty—that jobs were taken away in the process.

This community had true needs like access to clean water, job creation, proper nutrition, and school fees. If we are going to build healthy relationships, if we are truly going to have compassion, we then have to ask, how can I help my suffering friends flourish?

Mission trips are often self-centered. They are about the goer. Think about how wrong this is: "I'm going on a mission trip so I can be blessed and have an experience." Only rich Christians get to engage in this kind of missional activity. ("Rich" being relative, of course.)

This is a very thin, fine line; if done well, going on a trip can be amazing *if* you build long-term, healthy friendships and then partner with that community to unleash your human capital to solve tangible problems. Real lives will be changed, and it is beautiful and life giving for both the goer and the local community.

But if you go, have an experience, then leave and do nothing tangible, and if it costs so much money to go, and if it takes so much of the local community's time to host you . . . what have you really done? Have you helped more, or hurt more?

I've been "that" person. And it is okay to look back and realize that maybe we can learn from our mistakes, make some changes, do good, and do it well.

You can be deliberate and thoughtful, build powerful relationships, and help solve key problems as you return to visit your friends in this community, or you can be selfish, get your passport stamped repeatedly, upload some fun Facebook pictures of your trip, and have the experience of a lifetime. When it does nothing for the community you visited, it is nothing more than missional consumerism.

People matter; treat them well and short-term missions can be a tool to improve the world. We can do good, do it well, and do it with friends we care for.

# A Microloan and an Ice Cream Cone

I was in Zimbabwe in 2013 visiting John, his amazing wife Orpha, and all the kids. On this trip I also returned to that gas station for the first time—the gas station where God showed me I had to do *something*. It is a sacred place for me, and I was so excited to visit.

We had given out some microloans—small sums of money to help local individuals start small businesses—the year before, so we were visiting the recipients to see the progress of their businesses.

On the first stop we walked into a house with a box of chickens in the living room. This family had used a $300 microloan to start a chicken business. The family income had quadrupled in four months because of this new business opportunity.

After hearing their story and seeing the progress of their business, we said our good-byes. We walked out on the street making small talk. I asked the father how this made him feel to have his own business, to see his wife so excited to help run the family business, and to have more money to provide for their family.

I was expecting him to reply with something like, *"Our lives have been transformed forever."* Instead, in a very calm, smooth sort of way, here's what the father told me:

*"This loan has given us an opportunity and I'm very grateful. And what I love the most is that every Thursday I'm able to take my son to get an ice-cream cone. We've never been able to afford to do that before."*

In that moment so much of what we do made sense to me. We have fancy words and big data; it is all so overwhelming. Sometimes we get lost and we wonder if what we are doing is really working, if what we are doing really does matter.

And then a father shares a simple story. In that moment, this dad is like every other dad in the world. He loves his son and wants him to enjoy an ice-cream cone from the local market. He is like you and me.

# It's Not Easy Being a Spy

Two days after I met that boy at the gas station during my first trip to Zimbabwe, we were driving back to South Africa. Pastor John and his wife stayed home, so this drive consisted of my friend Steven, an American friend who had moved to Cape Town, and four other Americans. As we drove through Zimbabwe, we had to go through security checkpoints every hour or so. These checkpoints are always a bit nerve racking; you never know what is going to happen.

We approached another checkpoint and we were waved to pull over. A policewoman approached our van and peeked inside. Of course, I was such an idiot; I was wearing a camouflage hat (thanks, Willie). The policewoman made direct eye contact and quickly realized I might be a sucker, an easily cowed American. She proclaimed me to be an American spy and summoned me out of the van.

We walked across the dusty road where two other Zimbabwean police officers—men who seemed even less pleasant—were stationed.

"So, you are an American spy?"

"Who, me? No way!"

I mean, like most guys, I've always had visions of being James Bond. I quickly realized that those ideas are lame; being a spy is dangerous.

The officer told me that I was arrested on charges of espionage, I would spend the weekend in jail, and I would see a judge on Monday morning. I told him that I had a plane to catch in twenty-four hours and I could not go to jail. He looked at me as if I were an idiot, because, well, I was.

He demanded my passport; at that moment, I felt like I was already in prison in a foreign land, a place where the US embassy warned me they could not help if I were to get in trouble. Yes, I was on my own as a citizen.

Steven, who had lived in South Africa long enough to know how to handle this situation, was cool, calm, and collected. Every few seconds he would give me a look that said, "Marlow, just shut up and let me deal with this." I quickly glanced at the van as my friends watched all of this go down. One friend was crying, the other had his head between his knees praying, and my other friend was like, "Whatever—Steven will take care of it."

Steven began to share with the officers why we were in Zimbabwe. He mentioned Pastor John and the orphans and how we had come to help the kids of Zimbabwe. And just like that, something changed. The policewoman asked me if this was true, and of course I said, "Yes."

She started crying and explained that bribery is the only way they (the police in Zimbabwe) make money. The government was bankrupt and had no way of paying them. Then she told me her kids were living in a field close by and wanted to know if we *would take them to the orphanage so they would have a bed and food to eat.*

This is when I realized how vital compassion is, how vicious extreme poverty is, and why we should all care about those who are suffering. People are people. They are all loved by God and made in his image. And when we start to see that, well, it changes everything.

Suddenly I realized this policewoman has desires we all share—taking care of family, a safe place to sleep, food, and hope for the future—yet she was trapped in a broken system. She felt stuck right in the middle.

I was angry at this cop at first. But she taught me an invaluable lesson about injustice in that moment. I now understood her plight; my empathy went from zero to ten. She was a mom just trying to provide for her kids.

Thankfully, I was able to pay a fine for espionage of twenty dollars. In fact, the entire incident took less than five minutes. Steven will tell you I make all of this sound more dramatic than it really was, and maybe he is right. But I have not forgotten what I learned that day: what you see on the surface is not the entirety of the story, which is why we must correct oppression through the eyes of empathy. Was this officer wrong? Of course, but her poor decision making was caused by the suffering she and her family were experiencing. She was desperate and made a mistake.

The good news knows no borders. The church is a borderless movement; all who are created in God's image matter. And at our core as humans we share the same needs.

# Jesus, Compassion, and Calling

What I learned that day in South Africa is a new meaning of compassion, a word so often misunderstood. Compassion means to "suffer with." As I type these words, I cannot imagine a more important trait the world needs right now!

You cannot be a good neighbor without compassion. You cannot build a healthy society without compassion. Two of my favorite portions of Scripture show us the true heart of God.

Matthew 9 tells us that Jesus was going to cities and villages teaching the gospel and healing people of disease and affliction. Some of these people were suffering because of their sins, and others were suffering regardless of what they had done.

Folks who lack compassion are always chasing loopholes to avoid the responsibility to extend grace. They are looking for an easier life without admitting they took the easy route. Having compassion is hard; being judgmental is easy.

Jesus—he is a different kind of dude. He is a warrior with a tender heart, a man's man, but full of love and empathy. It all depends on which side of justice you are on!

> When he saw the crowds, he had compassion on them, because they were harassed and helpless, like sheep without a shepherd. (Matthew 9:36)

Jesus had compassion on the crowd. He could sense their pain and suffering. He did not demand them to change or be different (in this moment). He did not even have an opinion on *why* they were suffering. He just had compassion; it was as if he was also experiencing their brokenness and wanted to make them whole. We were all created to be whole, and Jesus is the only one who can fully understand what we were all meant to be and what we have become and how we can once again find our way back to wholeness.

Redemption is never too far away!

Jesus does not only tell his disciples to go serve the people; he had a bigger vision. He also tells his disciples to pray for *more* laborers. Jesus wanted *more* people to come and join the work of reconciliation and have compassion on those who were suffering.

You and I—we are the answer to that prayer. Their prayer still echoes into eternity. We need more people to get in the game, get dirty, and play to win so that we can help people thrive in those six key areas that we all desire.

You don't have to pray about it (*that is a loophole*). No need to fast about it (*another loophole*). You don't have to ask permission (*loophole*), and you don't even have to make sure the people you serve have checked all the proper theological boxes (*you guessed it: loophole*). You just have to say, "*Yes*! I'm in!"

We see Jesus' deep compassion again after another battle with the Pharisees. They love to create the loopholes as to why they're too good to follow the Jesus way and care for their neighbors who are not like them.

Jesus approached the city of Jerusalem, a city filled with its brokenness and pain. The passage reads:

As he approached Jerusalem and saw the city, he wept over it and said, "If you, even you, had only known on this day what would bring you peace—but now it is hidden from your eyes." (Luke 19:41–42)

Friends, please do not read this too quickly! Stop. Pause and process what this means for us. Our God wept over brokenness. This is a shared experience in Christendom. We are all called to weep when the good news is being overshadowed by bad news.

If there is one people group in the entire world that should be filled with crazy compassion, it is Jesus' people. Our God has extended mercy and grace; he has saved our souls from ourselves.

Just how, then, have we lost this sense of awe and wonder? In many ways Christianity is now better known for what we are against, when we should be known by what we are for: love, compassion, and justice.

Many so-called Christians are no longer for compassion; the brokenness of the world does not break them. These Christians would prefer to picket all of the world's problems. They want to be known more for what they're against rather than what they are for. They carry hate around like a weapon ready to destroy whoever is in their way. In their eyes, the world is black and white, and if you're on the wrong side, or even in the middle, you're an enemy not worthy of compassion until you conform to their views. They don't care about solving problems by showing love, having compassion, and seeking justice.

Often we Christians have become such bad news to those

outside of our faith that they cannot even fathom that we serve a gracious God who is full of compassion. In our fight for truth, we have covered up all the grace. For many, you have to be fully right or you are fully out. But those people are not my people, and those people are also not God's people!

We can prove truth by showing grace and being broken to a point where our compassion is so deep, our love is so strong, our willingness to lay down our lives for our neighbor, a stranger, the orphan, widow, or alien is so evident that folks have no possible way to avoid a love so deep and meaningful. They must face it head-on.

When they face it, they see compassion, which leads to repentance, which leads to redemption, which leads to even more workers who are in the fight, refusing to allow evil and suffering to win!

Christianity without compassion is like the NFL without a football, a Saturday morning with no cartoons, Chick-fil-A without chicken, or coffee without caffeine (coffee was *never* meant to be decaf).

I'm not interested in winning culture wars. I don't want to destroy people in the process of sticking up for truth. I refuse to be known as a person who hates another person or is better than another person for whatever reason.

When you are full of compassion and willing to love no matter the cost, truth will become evident. And when you stand for truth with a sense of humility and you have lived a life worth imitating, even those who disagree with you will respect you!

# Compassionless Christianity
# Is Unchristian

Lack of compassion tends to steer us to our own kind and creates harsh communities that thrive on judgment and lack empathy. In these communities hearts are hardened; the ethos of these communities breeds modern-day Pharisees.

On the other hand, compassion will help us to be vulnerable, which will then create a healthy posture of listening and learning and trying to understand the *why* before we try to *fix* everything. Vulnerability will create transparency. When we are transparent, we can have a sense of belonging in a safe environment.

We can begin to understand each other more. We have those deep conversations that bring to light what was once in the dark, and then something truly amazing happens. You begin to trust each other. You don't always agree or fully understand, but you begin to trust.

Trust will lead us to unity—this moment when you care more about the people than the cause. This shifts everything and builds a foundation for true transformation, even between people who may disagree on so many core issues.

Until we are unified, we can't make progress.

Why is the American government so dysfunctional?

Why are we so scared to get to know people who are different from us?

Why do we try to be the winner of an argument and make sure the other person is the loser?

Why is our world so conflicted and angry?

Why do we not care about "those" people over "there"?

Compassion is the starting point of transformation and doing good work and doing that work well.

# A Beautiful Friendship Begins

I will never forget the first time I stepped off the airplane and set foot on Haiti; the oppressive Haitian sun seared itself into my mind. It was May 2010—just four months after the massive earthquake had killed thousands of people in thirty seconds. The entire infrastructure of the country was wiped out. This place— just looking on the surface—would have been a prime example of the word *hopeless*.

I boarded a plane with my friends, storyteller Scott Wade and pastor Jacob Vanhorn. Together, we headed to Haiti in hopes of meeting some Haitian leaders. Our philosophy deeply believes that the local leaders, not outsiders, must create the future for their communities. We outsiders have a support role; we do not lead.

As we were planning the trip, we made calls to some friends who had a lot of experience in Haiti. We knew they could help us navigate the complexities and help us avoid making mistakes. Outsiders have made enough mistakes in Haiti, the ripple effect of which cannot be overstated.

Our hope was to find just one potential partner on this trip. The three of us knew in our hearts this was probably a long shot.

# A Leader to Lead Us

As I walked off the plane into an old, rickety warehouse with hundreds of other foreigners who were also coming to help, I was immediately drenched in sweat. I cannot tell you how much I hate to be hot, and this place was beyond hot. I felt like the heavens had lit an invisible flamethrower and focused it on this tiny island.

After two hours we finally were able to get through customs. We headed out of the airport, and my first glimpses of Haiti are still haunting. I had no clue that I would walk directly out into a makeshift tent city with hundreds of desperate people begging for help just outside the airport doors.

It is one thing to see suffering on a screen. It's quite another to look a man in the eye as you walk by and realize that he has no legs because of a thirty-second tremor. Men, women, and children . . . it was so difficult.

Our friends Jay and Jeremy picked us up, and I felt a sense of relief. As we drove off to our home for the next seven days, I felt as if I had just landed in a war zone. The UN seemed to be on every corner; there were tanks and trucks on the street and helicopters breezing through the Caribbean sky. Aid vehicles outnumbered Haitian vehicles. They all had their logos and trendy mission statements.

I was beginning to feel hopeless. Help One Now was broke. We had one staff member (me) and another person who basically volunteered part-time. I thought I had made a mistake. I wondered if we could truly help these people. I feared that our model would not make sense, and I had been told over and over that Haiti is a black hole for nonprofits. And of course, I was also a rookie in this game, green as could be.

But I believe in resurrections, second chances, redemption, and sovereignty.

After a sweat-soaked night of sleep filled with too many creepy crawlies and flying bugs, the sun brought me my first morning in Haiti. We met our driver and our translator; these young men were amazing. Their humility and strength and hope brought joy to my struggling soul. I would soon realize that it would always be Haitians who brought hope to their country—not some fancy plan created by an outsider.

We began our five-mile journey, which would end up taking over three hours. Collapsed buildings blocked the streets, and roads were twisted like hot metal that had just been torched with fire. But I was on my way to meet one of Haiti's great leaders; I just did not know it yet!

## Meeting a Hero

We were meeting five pastors at STEP, a local seminary. The school's president greeted us when we arrived. He walked us through the campus filled with young men and women who had a desire to be in ministry. We finally arrived at a small, grassy knoll where five other pastors—graduates of STEP—were sitting in a semicircle, waiting anxiously for us to arrive.

One by one they shared their story, their dreams for the future, and the heartbreak they had all been through.

As I listened to the stories, I feared these men were not the type of leaders we were seeking. This was the most important (and only) true meeting we had for the entire week. I kept asking myself, "What if none of these men fit the bill? What if we leave this meeting with zero opportunities?"

However, one of these pastors stood out. He was a quiet, humble man; he waited patiently while everyone else shared their stories. This man's smile and radiance drew my eyes to him. I would later find out he was a humble warrior-leader, and I would come to learn that he is one of Haiti's true heroes.

When it was time for Pastor Gaetan to speak, it was in an almost still, small-voice kind of way, in broken English and, at other times, in Haitian Creole. He began to unwrap the beautiful work he was doing. He was caring for fourteen orphans even before the earthquake. After the quake, neighbors in the community brought him kids whose parents had died or were so poor and devastated by the earthquake that they could not feed their kids.

He eventually turned children away as he realized that he could not help them all. He also shared his hopes for the future, the dreams still living in his heart.

I asked Pastor Gaetan what we could do and how could we help. He paused, looked down to the ground, then into my eyes. His words flowed directly from a broken heart

"You see, we have a problem in Haiti. We are lonely and life is so difficult. Each day I spend ten to twelve hours looking for rice and beans to feed the orphans. After the earthquake I had to officiate fourteen funerals. Most of my congregation have no jobs, no homes, and almost no way to survive; many of them live in tents.

"It's frustrating because foreigners keep coming to Haiti and you make us all of these promises. You say you will help us, help the kids, and help us get back on our feet. And then you leave and we never hear from you again.

"It's hard because I thought we would be friends and now I feel lonely because I never hear back from the people who visit. They see the kids, they attend our church, we pray together and dream together, they take our pictures. And then they disappear; that hurts me, and I've been hurt so many times that I can't take it anymore.

"All I need from you is to be my friend. I need to know that I'm not alone."

As Gaetan shared these words, my blood boiled and my heart sank. I could feel the pain this man had experienced and sense his soul becoming weary. He was in desperate need of friendship and partnership.

Jacob, Scotty, and I knew we had found one leader to spend more time with that week. God was leading us; maybe this was the breakthrough we needed.

# Living under a Tree

After the meeting Pastor Gaetan invited us to visit the orphans and meet his wife. He gave instructions to our driver, and a few hours later we slowly made our way to the Yahve Shamma Children's Home.

As we drove up to the gate, it slowly rolled open and we walked in. The stench of sewage from a canal parallel to the property filled the air. Pastor led us to the middle of this empty compound and under the shady relief of a massive tree. There were two tents; between them was an old hospital bed.

Gaetan and his wife slept in the bed. On one side was the tent for orphan girls, and on the other side were the boys. Gaetan said, "I am their shepherd; I sleep in between to protect the sheep." He introduced us to the kids; they were frail, made no eye contact, and had little to say.

Some had tears running down their cheeks, and their little bodies shook. This was my first encounter with orphans in Haiti. I felt as if I was back at that gas station in Zimbabwe, surrounded by thirty orphans, but this time I would not say no. This time I was determined to help.

Haiti was such a mess. I knew we could not help all orphans, but what if we could help these thirty-two kids and this one leader? What if we came back, again and again?

Pastor took us on a quick tour of the property. On one side were dozens of banana trees. We walked over to them, and suddenly he stopped in the middle of the trees and pointed down to a pile of dirt. On top of this dirt were one shoe and some flowers. It was his younger brother's grave.

He told us about his brother, who was attending business school at the local university. He was in class on the fourth floor. When the earthquake hit, the building pancaked and his brother died. When they recovered his body, he had one shoe; that shoe rested on his grave as a simple way to remember his life. Pastor Gaetan took out his wallet, removed a small picture of his brother, and handed it to me.

This man had lost so much, but he was a fighter who was not going to retreat!

He went on to tell us that he had an opportunity to move out of Haiti and live a more comfortable life in Arizona. But he could not leave these kids and his country. God had called him to stay and care for the orphans in Haiti.

I just could not fathom the pain and suffering that my new friend had endured. And yet, he did not ask for money or food; he simply asked for friendship. This was a guy who could lead us as we began to work in Haiti.

Jacob's small church, which had only existed for a few years and had fewer than eighty people, quickly decided to raise money to feed the kids. Meanwhile, we returned the following day to see the kids and listen to Gaetan's dreams. Today many of those dreams are fulfilled because our little crazy tribe of people decided we would return, over and over and over, and a small church filled with everyday, normal people who just gave what they could helped kick-start Gaetan's dream.

# The Power of a Garage Sale

A few months later we returned to Haiti. We had been in constant communication with Pastor Gaetan and had begun to help in small ways. I remember the moment we saw him for the second time as we drove up to the gate. His smile was unmistakable; he did a quick skip, like a kid who had just received some candy. We got out of the van and he gave us huge hugs; we were close friends reuniting.

Over and over we brought everyday, normal people—doctors and nurses, pastors and entrepreneurs, firefighters and dentists, IT professionals, stay-at-home moms, baristas, and even a bartender.

People like Don the dentist and Katie the child developer came. Together we rallied around Pastor Gaetan and the kids—not just for seven days but for 365 days. Every year. Once he knew we could help him feed his children, Pastor Gaetan started dreaming about a more secure place for his children to sleep. Regular people organized an event, Garage Sales for Orphans, and helped him build bunkhouses for the kids. When the children were safe and well fed, he was ready to dream about education. Pastor Gaetan is the leader; the rest of us serve him and ensure his vision comes ever closer to reality. We have laughed, prayed, cried, and even been angry with each other, but make no mistake, Pastor is one of heaven's heroes!

Doing good can be simple when you realize that doing good is always about people. The good news begins to have real, tangible impact when we commit to doing long-term good, good that shatters our selfish desire to travel the world and capture experiences and then disappear into thin air and break the hearts of the leaders who are trying so hard to make a difference. Yes, even mission trips can become an idol if they are full of selfish ambition and vain conceit.

## Phone a Friend

When I lived in Austin, we often went to live music shows—the heartbeat of Austin. One night, at a David Ramirez show, a friend in Haiti texted me. A massive windstorm had just struck Port-au-Prince and caused great damage.

I walked out of the show and called Gaetan. He answered the phone in panic mode. I asked him if he and the kids were okay. He said yes, though some of the kids almost died. They were still living in tents under the tree and a large branch fell onto one of the tents. Thankfully, Gaetan had moved the kids to a safer location just minutes before the branch fell from the skies.

If you were to ask Gaetan, this was the defining moment when he knew that our friendship was real, because I took the time to call him. *Relationships matter.*

We can't solve every problem in the world. We will never have enough money or time. But we can pick up the phone and ask if a friend is okay. This matters. It matters to our close family members, it matters to our coworkers, it matters to our next-door neighbor, and it matters to our friends across the world as well.

And this is why going global can be so good. We learn about each other. Yes, we have differences, and sometimes we will never fully understand each other's worldviews. That is okay. But when you drill down deep into the soul of every human, you will find that, at that core, we have certain desires that connect us to each other and cause us to pursue unity, seek peace, and hope that we all flourish.

## Six Desires of Every Human

We tend to view other people through our own cultural lens. We assume much based on our skin color, vocation, or geographical location. But when we peel away all the layers, we see more clearly that we're all so alike, so connected, and in need of the same basic necessities of life.

No doubt, some of us have been dealt a better hand than others. But no matter what cards you received, all of our basic needs are the same. Since we all have so much in common, it is far easier to focus on relationships and show compassion to each other. And compassion helps us to remember we are not so different after all.

*1. Purpose:* We all want to know we matter. We matter to God and we matter to each other. When we lack purpose, all sorts of negative outcomes come to life, like depression, suicide, and apathy. Some of the most depressed people I know are the richest people in the world. They lack purpose, and a life without purpose wreaks havoc on our souls.

We lose our way. We don't know why we get out of bed each morning. We don't understand how God can use our gifts for long-term good. We fail to realize we can build deep, meaningful relationships with one another.

When we lose purpose, we tend to focus on ourselves; this is when idols take hold. We drift toward a life of comfort, a life centered on our needs, wants, and desires. A purposeless life usually leads to a life that is not well lived.

2. *Opportunity:* I have sometimes felt stuck in life. Frustrated because, as much as I wanted to insist that I could fix everything on my own, Jesus was teaching me that he would prefer I learn how to trust him and be humble enough to seek help. When I think about community development and capacity building (fancy nonprofit words), I think first and foremost about opportunity. Here is what I have learned: For the most part, nobody wants handouts. They want help, but they want to be empowered. We all crave dignity.

We all want to chase an opportunity that might improve our lives and add meaning to our souls. The West is driven by this concept; we are dream chasers and risk takers. We strive to live the life we dream of, hope for, and desire.

So does the developing world. They're hungry for opportunities to improve their lives, care for their families, and transform their communities.

This is why foreigners can't be the center of the story. This is why we have to move from handouts, such as giving away old T-shirts, used toothbrushes (this happens, people), and the other silly things we do on mission trips that make the giver feel good and the receiver, terrible.

The question we must ask is, "What can I do to give someone an opportunity to thrive day to day?"

Think about this: God will use people like you and me to help other folks have a keen sense of purpose and meaning. They can flourish, their communities can flourish, and they can feel a sense of self-worth.

*3. Home:* Every human wants a home, a place to belong, a place to call their own. I do not mean just a structure; I mean a real home, a place of physical, and more importantly, emotional security. The world is filled with such chaos and confusion, and we're all busy and just need a place to Sabbath, a place to recollect our thoughts, a place to laugh, eat good food, and spend time with our loved ones and community.

We all need to feel safe in an unsafe world.

After the earthquake we started a project to build homes for Haitians who lost their houses and were living in tents. Each home created fifteen jobs for Haitians and helped families get back on their feet. These simple, 300-square-feet homes meant the world to a Haitian. It symbolized that they had a place to call their own, a community of neighbors to do life with, and an opportunity to flourish.

*4. Education:* Access to education is critical. Nelson Mandela stated in his 2003 speech, "Lighting Your Way to a Better Future," that *"education is the most powerful weapon which you can use to change the world"* (emphasis added).

I believe that to be true. An educated society will create a better future, a future that matters to all of us as we live in a global, interconnected world. When I visit our schools, I see the kids studying hard and joyfully while teachers and administrators do what they love to do. I can think of no greater way to bring sustainable change to these communities than by providing the best education possible to those who are trying to lift themselves out of poverty, chase their dreams, and have lifelong opportunities to thrive.

5. *Jobs:* Americans know that having a job is incredibly important. We are just now coming out of the terrible economic collapse that started in 2008. Unemployment hit double digits in some states; Americans panicked and assumed life as we know it was over. Let me juxtapose our heartache with some of the communities in which we serve, which have anywhere from a 40 percent to an 80 percent unemployment rate.

Most people in these countries survive in what is known as the informal economy. They work ten to twelve hours a day with one goal in mind: making enough money to buy food to feed their families at night. Just having food qualifies as a very successful day for billions of people in extreme poverty.

6. *Daily Needs:* Most of our friends around the world don't need a lot; heck, they do not want a lot. They do not care about all of the things that we in the West strive so hard to obtain. What they do need are the basics: clean water, nutritious meals, access to healthcare, and the time and opportunity to do life with family and friends.

When these basic needs are not met, a vicious cycle tends to take place. Desperation causes good people to do bad things in order to survive. And this is why it's vital that everyone be involved in poverty alleviation, because when we help people live a good life, they tend to enjoy life and not cause destruction locally and globally.

If folks are thriving, the chances that they will put on a suicide vest decrease. Joining a gang is no longer as glamorous; doing harm will fade as doing good will win.

As we build deep and meaningful relationships, keep these six desires in mind.

## Moments Matter

Every now and then I get to experience the moments that cause me to want to continue to fight. Whether I'm getting strong-armed by a mother desperate to feed her children by any means possible or seeing the impact of a $300 microloan on a father, I realize that we humans are more alike than we can possibly imagine. We all have the same core needs and desires in life.

What if doing good was simple? Well, it is. What if the good news of the gospel was truly good? Well, it is. Just ask the kid who is licking the ice-cream cone or a dad who has a job or a family who has a home or the fifteen workers who built that home.

Don't let the bigness of extreme poverty paralyze you. When our hearts are full of compassion, when we are thrilled to see the good news leak into culture, and when we commit to doing this kind of work the right way, we will see progress!

## — 6 —

# Good and Plenty

## *Everyone Has Something to Give*

We make a living by what we get;
we make a life by what we give.
Winston Churchill

Our friend and partner, Pastor St Cyr, started a church in the largest tent-city in Haiti—the same tent-city where we passed out whistles. Every time we visited Haiti, we worshiped there with our friends. I usually sat on the front bench on the right side of the stage. Almost always, little kids who love to play with us surrounded me. They gave us high-fives and hugs, they found a lap to crawl into and snuggle, and often, they asked for money while pointing to their bellies.

The band would begin to play. Drums would bang, the electric guitar would scream, and singers, whose lives were turned upside down by the earthquake, would lead us in worship with a sense of joy, enthusiasm, and passion that I can't fully comprehend. The sounds of pure, unadulterated love for Jesus poured through what seemed like the loudest speakers in Haiti. After worship, a short message of encouragement was usually shared, along with some testimonies, and then we closed in prayer.

One night we did not close as normal; instead, Pastor St Cyr shared his heart with his church. Of course, it was mostly in Creole. He quickly realized his non-Creole-speaking friends were out of the loop, so he paused and told us what was happening. Remember, this was less than one year after the earthquake. I was sitting with possibly the poorest people in the world; their homes were tents, and their beds were usually just rugs on top of earth. Each tent was like an oven baking in the heat of Haiti—a miserable way to live!

Pastor St Cyr was asking these people to give an offering so they could help start a church in the Dominican Republic. I was flabbergasted by this act of worship and generosity. I sat down, overwhelmed, with tears streaming down my cheeks. Honestly, it just made no sense to me. Surely, these people did not have to be generous in this moment of great suffering!

## The Ultimate Generosity Test

And to make things worse, they were being asked to give to people they generally dislike. Remember the story of the Samaritan and the Jew in Scripture? The two groups despised each other.

Haiti and the Dominican Republic are similar. They share an island, but they have a history of violence, war, and hatred. Yet these people in this tent-city—people who had lost *everything* while the Dominicans did not suffer at all from the earthquake—got out of their pews and walked down to the front of the stage to put money in the offering to plant a church in the Dominican Republic.

I realized that I was sharing a sacred moment, a moment that allowed me to see the power of dignity, sacrifice, and generosity in the flesh. I saw child-like faith. My faith would have found a loophole as to why I had an excuse—nay, a right—not to partake in this offering.

But Pastor St Cyr knew his community needed to feel part of what God was doing. They needed to participate in a larger story, and they needed the opportunity to know that God would use them to show the beauty of his kingdom. They still had to wrestle with what it means to love, serve, and be generous. No matter our outward circumstances, God is always focused on shaping our hearts and souls to be more and more like he created us to be!

# Called to the Impossible

Giving is powerful, and both the rich and poor are called to give. We are all called to love our neighbor and use our resources to do good. I remember talking to Pastor St Cyr as the service was ending. He told me the full story and how he wanted his people to focus on what it means to be used by God. This pastor was trying to bring health to the most important area of his people's lives—their souls.

I asked him how they could afford to give. How could he, as a leader, call them to do the impossible?

He told me that most of those who gave knew they would

have to fast a meal or even go a day without food to afford to give. They were giving until it literally hurt them; they had to sacrifice something important. These are the moments when I'm able to learn so much and see how beautiful and generous and giving people can be. Their faith was shaping my faith.

I also realized that any of us could make a difference, no matter our circumstances. Doing good is important for the health of the soul, which is far more vital than the health of a bank account. It shapes us into who God wants us to be, whether we are living in a tent in Haiti, a comfortable house in the United States, or a château on the French Riviera.

## Love Looks Like a Mattress

If you sponsor a child, have you had moments when you ask yourself: Does this even matter? It's a valid question, no doubt. But if you are sponsoring a child with a reputable organization, let me assure you that your money is making a big impact, just like the money from those Haitians walking down the aisle of the tent-city church.

After spending five days in Ethiopia, we were now in Uganda having dinner with Pastor Edward (our local partner) and his wife. It was a beautiful night and we were surrounded by beautiful people. I typically complain when I have to get on an airplane and leave my family, but these are the moments that make me love travel—enjoying good food with our local leaders and some great friends. It was a picturesque moment.

One of my friends asked Pastor Edward about the impact of child sponsorship. Without knowing it, Pastor Edward dropped the hammer on our peaceful dinner. My picturesque moment was shattered.

"Tomorrow when we go to the village, you will be able to tell who is in the sponsorship program and who is not. If they have a mattress in their room, you know they are sponsored. If the kids just sleep on the ground, you know they don't have a sponsor. Those kids also can't go to school and get an education!"

These moments crush me. Silence descended on the table as the reality of extreme poverty slapped our faces. Children sleep in the dirt because their families lack the resources to afford mattresses; their children cannot attend school because they can't afford school fees. Yes, it's frustrating and heartbreaking. Sometimes I want to scream, I'm so mad. My heart feels their pain. Yet, I know I cannot give up the fight to care for the poor.

## Celebrate Progress While Surrounded by Darkness

Then Edward, in his calm way of leading, said, *"You see friends, imagine if the Help One Now sponsorship program did not exist. Hundreds of kids would be sleeping in the dirt tonight, with nothing to eat. When they awoke tomorrow, they would also not be going to school. You're making a huge impact in my community. Thank you for your sacrifice!"*

I excused myself from the table and walked into the bathroom to compose myself. Tears had welled up in my eyes and my emotions were a little out of control. I was happy and sad; happy that God would use folks like us to serve kids in this community, but sad as I saw images of kids sleeping in the dirt while other kids have a mattress.

I reminded myself that I can't fix everything; that is not my burden (nor is it yours). That is God's burden to carry, but we were doing something that truly mattered. Hundreds of kids and families are being blessed and receiving care because hundreds of everyday, normal people are making a big difference by sponsoring a child. They are choosing to pause the busyness of their lives, see the pain of others, and respond by doing something that matters. We all have something to give.

## Have You Heard This One Before?

There's a story in the Bible that is all too familiar. As a matter of fact, maybe you check out when you hear it. Often that is what Scripture does for me; I've read and heard the same old stories so many times that a spiritual brain fog glosses over me. Even the most powerful stories in the world can become dull and lose their ability to transform if we don't protect our hearts and stay willing to allow the Jesus story to always be shaping how we live. Otherwise, we will drift off and allow apathy to lead our lives.

If you, like me, experience this spiritual fog, you know it is not good. So what do we do?

- Do we ask deeper questions?
- Do we just give up and assume we have conquered the sacred text?
- Do we feel that we no longer have to wrestle with the implications we're reading through?
- Do we read to check off a spiritual to-do list, and yet we bear little fruit?
- Do we go to church and just hope for the final amen so we can go to lunch, watch the game, mow the grass, or clean the house?

Or do we fight?

Or do we press in?

Or do we seek God until we experience a breakthrough?

I need you to fight. God needs you to fight. People who are suffering? They need you to fight. Do not allow the dominant culture to tell you how to live; allow the gospel to shape your thoughts and days, and live a life of purpose and meaning.

We can experience a breakthrough together. As you read this story, see it with fresh eyes and an open heart. I think you will be surprised by how much this story can shape your life and bring joy to your soul and purpose to your heart.

You are meant for so much. God won't force you to fight, but he will give you the power, tools, and strength to engage. But you have to make an effort; you must choose to stop and pay attention to those who are suffering!

# Why Being Generous Is Awesome

Critical, religious people constantly questioned Jesus. The more I lean into a gospel that defines seeking justice as a theological core value, the more I realize that some people will try any excuse to avoid engaging the poor.

A group of people gathered around Jesus, and a pious lawyer asked the Master Teacher a question that he hoped would create a loophole so he could continue to live a life that lacked mission and sacrifice yet ensured he had his ticket punched for eternity. He was looking for the easy way, but Jesus cannot be found down that road. Easy and simple are two different realities!

> Lawyer: "Jesus, what do I need to do to live on mission?"
>
> Jesus: "Love God and your neighbor; that's all."
>
> Lawyer: "Ok, cool, cool . . . so who is my neighbor?"
>
> Jesus: "Everyone who is created in God's image."
>
> Lawyer: "Um, I don't necessarily like all of those folks."
>
> Jesus: "But I do."

You see, this little paraphrase is why I wrote this book. This story is why I believe that "doing good is simple." It's true. And that means everyone—all of us—can do it. But, be careful not to misunderstand this to mean that doing good is *super easy*. Unfortunately, this is not the case.

Doing good can be simple, and it can be significant, but it will not always be easy. And that's why we need God's help every step of the way.

## Partner with God to Unleash Good

I believe ordinary people can partner with God, unleash good, change the world, and still have a life. We don't have to carry this heavy, impossible burden to fix all the world's problems—we just have to know where God has called us to help. You don't have to move to another country, quit your job, or stop enjoying life. This is not the mission or hope of Jesus; we are free in Christ, not trapped by religion.

The lawyer hoped that *simple* meant *easy*, as do many of us. But it doesn't. Simple means *clarity of calling*. Simple means we remove distractions and focus on impact. Simple to me means we don't try to change the world with our strength, wisdom, and power; we let God do all of that. But we do try to change the world with the gifts that he has given us and by choosing to stop and love the needy.

Jesus shares the parable of the Good Samaritan for a reason. He is trying to shape how we humans will live after he departs and heads back to his heavenly home. He wants us to grapple with what it means to love well, with who can make an impact, and with how they can make an impact.

This story is about an everyday, normal person who said yes to an opportunity to help someone who was suffering. The Levite and the priest, who were religious leaders and should have known to show compassion because of their belief in a loving God, did not. These men, who studied and taught the Scriptures and knew the words of Isaiah 1:17 intimately, chose to ignore the suffering of the beaten man on the bloody path.

God, however, will use anyone at any time; such is the case with the Good Samaritan. As far as we know, he had no real titles or position of power. He was just a guy going about his day-to-day life. But his heart and soul were healthy and he cared about his fellow man, even if that man was an enemy. Soon an opportunity to care would show up! His actions would change the course of history, and his story would become the model of generosity for the rest of eternity.

This Samaritan was traveling the Jericho Road. This path was dangerous; it was also known as "the bloody way." Many thieves hid out in this mountainous terrain to try to take advantage of sojourners on their travels.

The Samaritan was not a god nor the Son of God; he was not an apostle or even a disciple following Jesus. As far as we know, he was normal in every sense of the word. He could have been a doctor, carpenter, or entrepreneur. He could have been wealthy, middle-class, or even poor. We have no backstory, other than that he was from the dreaded place of Samaria. Yet he did what the religious people in this story refused to do when an opportunity came his way.

I believe that Jesus was using the parable of the good Samaritan to teach his people how to be brave enough to take action when needs become evident. The Samaritan showed compassion, used his own money, took time out of his busy schedule, risked his life, and cared for his neighbor. This was not a mission trip or planned event; the Samaritan was committed to compassion, service, and generosity within his own day-to-day rhythms of life!

The priest and Levite, on the other hand, were too busy or afraid to stop. Maybe they did not care, or maybe they did not want to touch a dead man. If they did, they would be excluded from religious activities for seven full days, according to tradition. But then again, is this not what made God upset in Isaiah—when a disciple chose religion over people?

If so, we do know that they missed the point of what it means to be a God-fearing person. And, to be honest, I've been in their shoes more times than I want to admit. I look the other way when I walk by the homeless; I ignore the children in my community who have needs that I can meet.

Often I see the broken and I just keeping walking. I try to tell myself that I did not see it, but I know I'm lying to myself, searching for that loophole so I don't have to sacrifice or deal with an inconvenient moment. I have learned that Christianity is often inconvenient. But Jesus calls us to love our neighbor while he offers us the grace we need to give *something*.

For instance, before I met the boy in Zimbabwe, I was the modern-day Levite and priest in this story. I was too busy to stop and help; I had sermons to prepare, business meetings to attend, Sunday services to plan.

Of course, it was all in the name and mission of Jesus.

If I wanted, I could have hid in the church office all day long, created some blog posts on what it means to be on mission, booked meetings with church people, then studied the Bible more and attended another small group. *I could have used religion to avoid mission all day long.* In fact, I think it's safe to say that millions of Christians are doing just that.

I could have avoided the dangerous pathways altogether. If so, I would never have had the chance to see the broken. That vision would never have the opportunity to shape my soul; then I would have never experienced the redemption. When a broken person is made whole—and remember, God uses normal people to be part of that process—life has meaning beyond our grasp.

Doing good and loving your neighbor will look different for all of us. We may or may not walk down the most dangerous paths in the world, but hopefully we will be willing if that is what God asks us to do. However, we can still live dangerous lives and truly help people who have been left for dead—the single mothers who are struggling to raise their kids, the parents down our streets who have lost their jobs, the orphans who live in abandoned gas stations, the foster kids who are desperate to belong to a family.

## The Heart of God Is to *Give*

God is good because God is a giver. He gave us the earth and all of its wonders. The sunrise on the Outer Banks of North Carolina is awe-inspiring; hiking the mountains of Appalachia is breathtaking; watching the leaves turn colors every October is magical. God gave us the gift of nature and beauty.

God gave us each other. My wife and kids are such a blessing. Occasionally I look at all I have and I can't help but be thankful. I'm a kid from a trailer park. My family life as a kid was so fractured, it is impossible to even explain the depth of brokenness. Yet God reached out to me and began a marvelous work. He gave me life and forgiveness and purpose, and he also gave me a family to love, care for, and lead, and friends who love and support me. I've experienced redemption, and it was—and is—beautiful. And I want others to have the same experience!

God gave us gifts, and they bring meaning and purpose to our souls. These gifts create a world full of wonder, a painting that seems impossible to look away from, a song that brings tears to our eyes and joy to our hearts. These gifts can create a book that captivates us and causes sadness when we reach the last page and realize the journey is over, and we don't want it to be over because the journey has been wild and fun and joyful.

God has gifted some of us to be entrepreneurs, social workers, nonprofit leaders, teachers, and accountants. These gifts create work that matters to the world. They are good and plenty.

We could go on and on, but what is important is to realize that God gifted us so we can use those gifts to make the world whole. Your gifts were always meant to serve your neighbor well. They are not always flashy, but they all matter. As I write this, a plumber is in my home fixing a broken water pipe. For three days dishes piled up while we have been unable to use the dishwasher. Trust me: this plumber's gifts matter to my family!

God also gave us Jesus. Some of you may not agree; for you, this may seem crazy to even imagine, but stick with me. I want you to know what I know to be true in my life. Deep in my heart, I believe that I was a sinner far from God. But God gave the world a gift. He sent his Son to teach us how to live and then to die on an old rugged cross.

God was so generous that he gave his Son so that my soul can be saved and made whole, and so that redemption could have flesh in lives that are fully transformed.

To me, this is the greatest gift that has ever been given to me. It reveals the simple fact that we serve a God who loves to give gifts. Scripture tells us that *God gives gifts to those who ask (Matthew 7:11)*, and that *every good and perfect gift comes from above (James 1:17)*.

If God is a giver, then his people should also be known as givers, yes? It seems difficult to say, "I follow Jesus," and not really mimic who Jesus was—a giver.

As a matter of fact, God warns us in 1 Timothy 6:17–19:

Command those who are rich in this present world not to be arrogant nor to put their hope in wealth, which is so uncertain, but to put their hope in God, who richly provides us with everything for our enjoyment. Command them to do good, to be rich in good deeds, and to be generous and willing to share. In this way they will lay up treasure for themselves as a firm foundation for the coming age, so that they may take hold of the life that is truly life.

You were created to use your gifts to do good works, or, as Timothy would say, you are commanded to do good. When your soul is healthy, when giving becomes a passion, you will then be able to also do what the Good Samaritan did. You will be willing to stop when an opportunity comes your way to use your gifts and resources for redemptive purposes!

## Givers Because We've Been Given To

God commands us to do good. He does not even give us an option. This may sound harsh to you; I know it can be easy for us to despise being told we have to do something. This is when pride enters our hearts and creates a soul that is not willing to love, serve, give, and help. Sadly, it is easy for millions of Christians who faithfully attend church week after week not to live in such a way that they are compelled to give (or even care).

When that happens, we focus on building our kingdom, using our resources and gifts for our own good, not the common good of the world. The injured Jew is just a hassle whom we ignore along the way!

This is not just anyone commanding; this is God, the ultimate Giver, who is filled with immeasurable grace and love that can never fully be understood or grasped. God wants you and me to do good because he is good and he knows that if we are generous, we will also be better off for it.

God wants you and me to be *rich*, not by how much money we have in the bank or how big our homes are or how successful people say we are but by our good deeds. This is, of course, why some of the richest people in the world are materially poor while the poorest people in the world are materially wealthy.

Why is this so critical? Because it is not just about to *whom* you are being generous. It is also about *you*. Generous people can look in the mirror and feel a sense of joy and peace, knowing we are using the blessing of God to help bless others. Generosity is a sign that our souls are healthy; this brings great joy to God and great meaning to us.

A generous person knows that wealth has not become an idol, but that our gifts are being used to bring glory to God. A generous person has chosen to build a different kind of kingdom, because a generous person knows that wealth and possessions can never fully satisfy.

Living an others-focused life and serving God is a better way to live. It is a better way to raise your family; it is a better way to spend your days. They go fast; live generously and make an impact!

## Hope Matters

Maybe you look at the nightly news and see the world's brokenness. It is not hard to see how messed up the world seems to be. I mean, it has always been this way, but I think we would agree that technology has advanced how much evil we see daily. Social media has created a platform of nonstop communication to a point where it's exhausting even to try to process all the information, much less to try to figure out how to make a difference—especially as we try to juggle life's day-to-day demands. Friends, this is hard, but you do not have to be amazing at everything all the time. It's okay to wrestle with the brokenness and what you are supposed to do.

One thing I do know is this: God has called his people to be a community that brings hope to the world because we have found hope in the good news of the gospel—hope that has healed our souls and transformed our lives. We have to be careful that this good news does not become dull, lest we forget the great blessing and responsibility that comes with being a disciple of Jesus.

Yes, we see never-ending acts of violence, terrorism, unimaginable suffering, and greed. It can be suffocating and debilitating for so many that I wonder how we can stop this tide of darkness and evil. But the good news is this: God uses people like you and me to fend off evil. Like Erwin McManus said, "He burdens the heart that he calls."[1]

Embracing the depth of God's love and generosity will change how we view the world and the evil that exists. We can focus our efforts on being light, so the darkness must run and hide and no longer exist. Leading Help One Now has allowed me to see everyday, normal people do this exact thing.

Darkness is running from the light—the light that is the

good news. The good news spreads when God's people decide that evil has had enough. To me, there is simply nothing more powerful than a local church that asks her people to live on mission together, a church that chooses to be light in the darkness of society, a church that helps their people use their gifts to do good, do it well, and do it together.

# A Generous Church

There are churches like this all over; one is Austin New Church (ANC). My friends Brandon and Jen planted this church deep in the heart of South Austin. The first time I visited, I recognized their drummer. He was a homeless man who played on a white bucket on Sixth Street (one of Austin's most well-known areas), asking passersby for change.

When Hurricane Ike hurled through Houston in 2008, ANC decided to do something; they determined to be generous. In moments like these, prayer alone will not suffice; *doing good always lives in the tangible.* The city of Houston was in shambles and needed help, so ANC rallied a bunch of churches in Austin and began to take down supplies to churches in Houston, each and every day, for weeks.

Trailers were rented and donations were given. But their generosity did not stop there. ANC's members opened their homes for the Latino community in Houston. Yes, it is risky to take strangers into your home, but when did God ever call his people to crave safety?

I know that at one point, Jen and Brandon had over twenty people who lived in their home for nearly a month. The church as a whole had over eighty people who temporarily moved from Houston to Austin until they could get back on their feet. It was a simple (though certainly not *easy*), tangible way that they could help those whom life had beaten up.

What if doing good was simple? It is; it can be as easy as opening your home or taking a three-hour drive to help others or gathering supplies for strangers who become friends. This is a modern-day version of living like the Good Samaritan—doing good deeds to those who are hurting.

## Driving into the Fire

I told you earlier that our church, Vista, had become part of the Austin Stone. One day a tragic apartment fire ignited in Austin's St. John's neighborhood, a community that struggled with poverty. Austin Stone had become intentional about serving this community. They started to mentor kids at the local high school and to work with stay-at-home moms and refugees. They did not try to fix everything; they just began to build relationships.

Hundreds of people lost everything that day. Twitter exploded with the news, and some of us were trying to find a practical way to help. My friend Stew began to rally the Austin Stone community within a matter of minutes. Other local churches also started to help.

Soon hundreds of people across the city of Austin were driving toward the fire with life-giving supplies like formula, diapers, water, food, and clothing. I gathered my family, told them what was happening, and we went shopping. We loaded our car with essential supplies and picked up more from other friends who wanted to help.

As we drove to a dedicated triage point, we passed ambulances and police vehicles and saw firefighters courageously fighting the blaze. It was a bit hectic, but the neighborhood had come to a standstill. Families were lying on the grass, watching what little that they had burn away.

So many Austinites wanted to help; it was such an encouragement to see people caring for those who were hurting. We finally found a place to park. I stood for a moment as I watched the flames still burning. My family gathered the water, diapers, and other supplies and took them inside.

One of the firefighters was resting on the grass, and he asked me what was happening. Why were all of these people coming to the fire? Usually people try to get away. I told him that we heard about the fire through social media and were coming to provide immediate resources. We had quickly realized that the local churches would arrive before the Red Cross, and isn't that how it should be?

While we could not fix everything that day, we were able to do something that mattered in that moment. Not only was I able to help, but my entire family was involved. Yes, it was a bit inconvenient. Like the Good Samaritan, we had to stop what we were doing, we had to use our own money (from our small savings account), and I even had to take a dreaded trip to the grocery store. But we did good, did it well, and did it together. Real people who were going through real tragedy had relief.

In the next twenty-four hours, my friends at the Austin Stone found a temporary place for everyone to live, and they worked with the city to find permanent housing for many as well.

This is what it means to be generous: to do good and to be a neighbor. To give what you have.

New City Life has done just this. This church funded the initial project for our work in Haiti, all through the generosity of normal people giving what they have. They also run what is called the re:work project. Local homeless folks come to their church and learn a trade such as woodworking. They make and sell birdhouses, cornhole games, and tables. The homeless are able to work and make money so they can live.

If a church is focused on being generous and activating their people to unleash good locally and globally, the amount of impact they can have is off the charts. The great tragedy is when a church decides to build an empire and focus on how many people are coming on Sunday as opposed to how many people the church is sending out to serve locally and globally!

## Paralyzed by the Dark

It's always exciting when you feel that life has purpose and meaning. I love that I'm able to see tangible hope and real lives changed and transformed because of the generosity of others.

One of the reasons we get paralyzed is, all the brokenness seems too big to repair. We can't microwave these problems with quick fixes or just slap them with Band-Aids. Add to that our fast-paced culture, and often we are just trying to manage our own chaos. We do not feel like we have the time or mental energy to do good, so we don't.

I've been there. It's okay—as long as we don't stay there! I'm hoping this book will be a tool that will help compel you forward without weighing you down with a burden you were never called to bear.

In the case of the St. Johns fire, I had a role to play: give supplies and rally other people to do the same. Lives of real people were impacted. Other folks—the experts—did the key hard work. I was able to help them accomplish the work.

Most of you do not have to get into the nitty-gritty. You do not have to rebuild collapsed infrastructures, create better sanitation systems, or solve the food crisis. That may not be your role. You may not be an expert, nor do you have the time or capacity.

## Just Start with One

In Haiti the unemployment rate hovered around 70–90 percent in 2011. It was an overwhelming figure. Where do you start? Whom do you help? Does it even really matter? The problem is just so big.

I can't create millions of jobs, but what if I could help create five or ten or twenty? We just need to start somewhere.

Thankfully, our local partner in Haiti and good friend, Jean Alix Paul, is basically a legend. He had a handful of people he trusted and knew could start businesses.

Richard was one of those guys. He is an artist, married, and the father of a young son. Their home was destroyed in the earthquake, and they were among the first community members to get a new home built for them. When we build new homes, we do it so the family can add on to their homes if they are able. Our hope is always to help them build a foundation, to give them a place to start.

With his family safe in a home, he was able to paint all the time. He sold his painting to vendors all over Haiti. I was talking with him one day and asked about his business. One of the reasons he was not able to grow quicker was that he had no access to capital. He had a gift, he worked really hard, he knew how to sell, but still he was not able to generate enough revenue to put back into his business.

So I told Richard that we had a donor who wanted to give him a business loan for $500, which was enough to provide him with the supplies to produce over one hundred paintings. Richard would give us fifty pieces to sell in Raleigh, and we would split the proceeds. Half would be Richard's profit, and the rest would be used to build additional homes in his community.

Two months later, we were back in Haiti and I saw his thriving business. He had dozens of paintings fully finished, and he was making more revenue than ever. We picked up our fifty paintings, sold them at the art show, and made enough to begin construction on two more homes in Haiti.

A few weeks after Christmas in 2011, I was back in Haiti. I walked up this little hill and followed the dirt pathway to Richard's home. I had a white envelope with roughly $2,500 that Richard had earned from the art show.

Richard, his wife, and his little boy gathered just outside his home. I handed him the envelope and told him it was his earning from the art show. He opened the envelope and began to count cash. His eyes became wide as tears streamed down his cheeks. His wife was a little confused as she watched him counting.

We explained to her that all the money was theirs. Richard commented on the amount of money and that they had already paid the loan back. He told her that *all* of the cash in that envelope was theirs and just like that, she collapsed onto the wall of her house for a moment. She could not fathom that all the money in the envelope was their earnings.

Richard hugged me and kept saying, "Thank you, thank you." I told him that he was the one who had the skills. He used those skills to provide for his family and to raise money for another family in his community to move out of a tent and into a home.

A year later, Richard has now tripled the size of his home. He has a thriving art business, and he is a leader in his church and community. This happened because one person decided to give $500 to help launch this business.

When Richard repaid the loan, we used these funds to help another entrepreneur launch a business. A year later, he repaid the loan and doubled his business revenue. We took that loan and helped another person launch another business.

What if doing good was simple? In fact, sometimes it is so simple that it seems too good to be true. But it just shows us how we can all work together. Jean Alix is a high capacity local leader; he knew Richard would be able to use the funds well. Help One Now had spent much time in this community developing a model that would make an impact, and then a donor stepped in and gave. Now hundreds of people have been blessed, jobs have been created, and families are thriving.

In 1 Timothy, Jesus commands us to do good because he knows that generous people will help solve problems and make the world a brighter place. I think we can all agree—we need the light to shine to overcome the thick, overwhelming darkness. And sometimes it can start with the simple act of giving what we have.

# 7

# All Great Things Start Small

## *How to Stage a Movement*

If I cannot do great things, I can
do small things in a great way.
Martin Luther King Jr.

Have you seen the video from Seattle's 2009 Sasquatch! Music Festival, "Guy Starts Dance Party"?[1] It starts on a grassy hill, where a crowd of people are listening to an artist named Santigold perform. Everyone is sitting, except for one guy. He is . . . letting the music move him. People are laughing, but he is not worried. He is just there having fun.

Finally, people start to join him. The first guy to come is a bit awkward, and the crowd mocks him. He has to have some sort of Pentecostal background, like me. I've done some crazy dancing in church when I was a bit younger (thankfully, before social media existed)!

Dancers two and three are even more awkward. We quickly

realize that these dudes should not be dancing in public; this is not what they were gifted to do. Honestly, you can only get away with dancing like that at a festival, and possibly only if you enjoyed two, four, or maybe twenty of a certain type of beverage. But these three guys are brave, or stupid, or drunk—or some combination of all three.

Soon a few more flock to the dance party, and then a few more, and then the tipping point happens and dozens flock from all directions. The crowd cheers as hundreds are dancing in this carefree moment of pure joy and simple silliness. The point is that one person was brave: he started a party and created memories that will last forever.

I'm assuming this guy had no clue he was being filmed, and of course he had no idea that his one-man dance party would go viral on YouTube. As I write this, over 12.5 million people have seen this clip. Many major motion pictures don't get that many viewers.

## A Scary Awesome New Road

Being generous is brave. Caring for our neighbors requires bravery. But being brave is scary. Most of us are trying to figure life out as it comes; we are looking for trailblazers to show us a way forward. Why else would we shop at IKEA, drink Starbucks coffee, or order a double double (Animal Style, of course) and Instagram that bad boy as quick as we can?

We tend to follow the crowd; it gives us a safe place to learn life. But we all have to ask this: Where exactly is the crowd taking us? Are we sure we want to go down that pathway, or is there a better way?

I believe Jesus shows us a better way. The better way may require us to go down the road less traveled, though. It's not quite as safe; that road requires something from us. We may stick out a bit, but that is good. Others will follow when we decide to stick out for the right reasons!

I want to be a part of a movement that is committed to doing good, and I hope you do too. Together we can have a global dance party, invite people to join us, and make the world brighter. It is the only way forward.

## One Step Forward

Give, and it will be given to you. A good measure, pressed down, shaken together and running over, will be poured into your lap. For with the measure you use, it will be measured to you.

*Luke 6:38*

When I returned from Zimbabwe, I wrestled with how to help those kids in a tangible, real way. I remember one moment of clarity as I was walking in my garage, looking at everything we had stored and how the majority of stuff was never used.

Maybe you can relate as well. I had the exercise bike but not the six-pack abs. There were the bins of old clothes, stuffed animals with only one eye (people will buy those, you know), unread books, and more. I also began to scope out my friend's garages and saw the same thing.

It's amazing how much valuable junk we have stored up in our garages. I thought, maybe this junk could be repurposed for good?

I began to research storage units; what I found out was amazing. Americans love to spend hundreds of dollars a month to store up the extra stuff they never use. Stop for a moment and think about this: we spend hundreds of dollars a month to store stuff we don't really ever use. That is real money, wasted.

Over \$24 billion[2] is spent annually on storage units. Some of this makes sense; we move and need a place to store our stuff for a season. What flabbergasted me was how many folks just use these units as a third or fourth garage.

In 2013 the Self Storage Association released a study with the following facts:[3]

- 1 in 10 households in the US currently rent a self-storage unit.
- There are over 59,000 self-storage facilities in the world. Over 48,000 are in the US.
- Total self-storage rentable space in the US is now 2.3 billion square feet. That figure represents more than 78 square miles of rentable self-storage space—or an area more than three times the size of Manhattan Island.
- It took the self-storage industry more than 25 years to

build its first billion square feet of space; it added the
second billion square feet in just 8 years (1998–2005).

The question we really need to ask is this: "When is enough,
enough?" How much more do we really need, and why are we
consuming so much? It is hard for those who struggle with consumerism to be generous; it is hard to walk down the narrow path.
But I think we could all agree—living out the good news requires
examination of all facets of our lives. Of course, we will all find
areas that we need to work on, but remember—grace wins!

As I studied the storage industry and our model of "Doing
Good Is Simple," I was determined to create tools so that anyone
could get involved and make a difference. I did not want people
to feel like the only way they could help was to write checks.

## Yes, One Person Can Start a Movement

In 2009 I was a big-time blogger. Usually I had like forty to fifty
people who would visit my blog. Big-time! My platform was
rapidly expanding. Twitter and Facebook were gaining lots of
traction, yet they were still small enough not to be overwhelming.
Back then, you actually connected with people on social media,
and often they became your real-life friends.

So I started asking people to throw garage sale parties and
donate the proceeds to help care for the orphans in Zimbabwe.
The economy was literally falling to pieces, and I was desperate
to create simple but powerful ways for folks to get involved. I had

no idea whether this would work, but then something beautiful happened.

A church in Pennsylvania began to dance with us. Online friends Nathan and Courtney had followed my journey. They decided to have the college and career ministry of their church do a two-day garage sale. I had no clue they were doing this until I went to pick up the mail one afternoon.

At this stage in the game, going to my post office was usually depressing. We would go weeks without any donations. Often my bank would email me that we did not have enough cash in our business account to keep it open.

But this day would be different. I grabbed the mail and followed my regular routine; I headed back to the car and sorted the letters. Of course, one was more unusual than normal. I opened the envelope and I saw a check made out to $4,000 with this note from a pastor: "Hey Chris. Some of our college and career students saw you post something on Twitter. They did a two-day garage sale and raised some funds for your mission. We are so thankful to be part of what you are doing and glad we could help."

I was stunned. An idea I had was now wrapped in flesh. I called this pastor, and he was excited that his church had a way to get involved and help serve orphans. He was also excited because he was able to connect with his local community and share why they were doing all of this hard work to throw a garage sale.

They were the first people to dance; they are proof that one can start a movement that can do good and do it well. I remember sending the proceeds of that garage sale to Pastor John in

Zimbabwe. The relief we both shared created a deep bond and trust. He was fighting to care for the kids every day, we were fighting to give him resources so he could get the job done, and now this random church had decided to dance with us and raised enough money to help the orphans for months.

A few months later my friends at Austin New Church did a church-wide garage sale Sunday. Every fifth Sunday of the year, they don't go to church service; rather, they go serve the community. That Sunday they asked all of their missional communities to throw a garage sale party.

And they all went *big*. Multiple large garage sales were happening all over the city of Austin.

Brandon sent me a text later that evening. He told me they had raised $12,000 and wanted to fund the water-well project in Zimbabwe. That project still works and thousands of people in Zimbabwe have been drinking clean water. The kids in Zimbabwe now had food and water, all because two churches danced with us.

Then we started having small groups, families, friends, and strangers all doing garage sale parties. Each week, more cash would trickle in with a note.

I remember a church in Compton, California, sending me a check and thanking me. They did a garage sale and raised $300 for orphans. Their pastor had told me they had never really known a good way to give back to orphans as they had so many challenges in their own communities.

My friends Adam and Stephanie have thrown annual garage

sale parties and raised over $20,000 in the last three years. The first party was their own excess, but for the second, third, and fourth they asked their friends and neighbors to donate their stuff. Those neighbors brought their stuff over before the garage sale; Adam and Steph stored it and then sold it.

This is the beauty of the movement. Adam and Steph loved to see their kids involved, and they got excited to ask their neighbors to participate and help care for the poor. Many of their neighbors are well off, and they get asked to donate money *all* the time. But this is a different way to get them involved with their entire families.

Yes, it requires work and sweat, but the payoff is seeing lives changed.

Help One Now used the proceeds to fund key projects. Kids were being fed, clean water wells were being drilled, and homes were being built for Haitians living in tents.

This early success taught me this: Most folks want to help. They want the world to be better, but often they just don't want to be the first one at the dance party. They don't know *how* to get involved. Yes, we can write checks, which are powerful and amazing.[4] But, being generous has to go deeper than writing checks.

## Small Is the New Big

Movements are everywhere. Usually a movement is started because a problem exists. Some movements shape the entire world and are written in the history books, while other movements last for a season and then disappear. Some movements do good and others do evil. The hearts of the people determine the outcome of the movement.

- Jesus started a movement known as Christianity.
- The antislavery movement was launched in the United States in the late eighteenth century.
- Martin Luther King Jr. and others started the civil rights movement in the 1950s.
- In the 1800s a movement was launched to ensure women have equal rights.
- ISIS started a movement to establish an Islamic state.
- The Taylor Swift movement has enveloped teens and tweens everywhere. (And, by proxy, their parents. As a dad of two teenagers, I have little choice but to be involved in the Tay Sway world.)
- Crossfit is a movement for fitness freaks. I went to a class recently, and I had no clue I could breathe that hard. I mean, I could not walk for a week!
- Craft coffee, beer, wine, cocktails, and cheese are having their movements as well.

In 2011, we moved from Austin, Texas, to Raleigh, North Carolina. I love Austin; it's like my second home. I miss it—the music, the breakfast tacos, the people, the breakfast tacos, the local vibe, and the breakfast tacos. But we needed to expand Help One Now and we chose Raleigh.

Now I live, work, and play in downtown Raleigh, and I absolutely love my city. Over the last decade, Raleigh has launched a movement to "eat and shop local." The stickers are everywhere; as residents, this became important to the core of who we are. We love our community and want to give back to the people who live here. The human connection is deep, and we want to support one another.

I spend a lot of time working and writing at local coffee shops. You will usually find me at BREW in Raleigh, drinking a yummy cappuccino crafted by my good friend AJ. The coffee they serve is from Raleigh Coffee Company—my friend Joe owns that roastery. The milk they use is from a local farm, and the bread they use comes from Yellow Dog Bakery—right down the street.

I also go to Jubala because my friend Andrew is giving back to coffee farmers all over the world. I do a lot of shopping at the neighborhood market and bakery; I consume food at restaurants where I know the owners and their stories. When I spend money, I'm investing in them because I believe in them and the impact they have on my city.

This was not always the case, but one day a group of citizens decided to launch an "eat local" movement. And this movement is not just here in Raleigh—dozens of other cities are doing the same. I'm just following someone else's lead. But I'm thankful because I believe this to be a good thing for society. And that's how big movements always begin: with ordinary people taking small steps.

Of course, it goes far beyond coffee and spontaneous dance parties.

# A Trafficking Story
# You Have Never Heard

In 2011 we began a conversation with our local Haitian friends and community leaders. Trafficking of people had become a big issue in Haiti, and we knew something had to be done. Kids were being sold over the border in the Dominican Republic. It is haunting and tragic. One day we gathered leaders from this border community—the mayor, police chiefs, judges, clergy, and anyone else who was interested.

I shared about the global issues of human trafficking. Then I told some local stories I had heard. Heads began to bob; these people knew human trafficking was happening in their community. After I finished my ten-minute talk, Pastor Jean Alix shared in Creole like a fiery prophet who was speaking the heart of God to the people of Israel.

It was a hot day, and sweat poured from his brow. He demanded action and told everyone that his church would help; this was real and kids were being sold into slavery. This was a "Martin Luther King Jr." moment for this community. Pastor Jean Alix was basically saying, "I have a dream that trafficking will not be allowed in this community, and I'm willing to work to see that dream become real." I was on the front row, so I could not see when a hand had raised from the back. All heads turned; the mayor had stood up and began to share his story and the realities of trafficking in this community.

Quietly, the Haitian government was rescuing kids. The

border crossing into the Dominican was unprotected and wide open. Kids would be sold and taken off to the labor fields, sold to families for servitude, or sent to brothels to be used as sex slaves. The crowd was angry; you could sense their hearts being broken. This conversation had been taking place in the dark for years, but now it was in the light.

After the meeting was over, the mayor walked up to me, put his hand on my shoulder, and told me that he had many children who now lived in the local prison because he had nowhere to take them. These kids were rescued at the border, but the government had no infrastructure or system to help them.

He asked if I could go pick them up and care for them. I was stunned by what he had just told me. "Kids in prison because they had been rescued?" I told him that I could not, but what I would do was help him solve this problem long term.

We had an idea that we believed in and thought would work, so I shared it with him. I told him we could build a community center with multiple houses. Each house would have a house mom who was committed to caring for rescued kids. A school and a church already existed, but we could add a preschool, a clean water project, a medical clinic, and more. I even told him we could start a job-training program, as much of trafficking takes place because of the issues that extreme poverty creates.

I told the mayor that if he would rescue the kids, we would have a place for him to bring them.

It would be a center led and staffed by Haitians, Haitians who are fighting human trafficking every day. The mayor was so grateful. I could sense his shame and frustration. He wanted to help, solve a problem, make a difference. He just could not do it alone.

I remember the moment I got a call from Jean Alix six months later. I was in my office in downtown Raleigh. He said we had taken in four kids. Those four kids became nineteen, and the nineteen became one hundred. Some will live in this community and be raised, as they no longer have families. Others will be reunited with their families.

One day Lamar, our international operations director, called and told me the story of a little boy they had just rescued. Like many of the kids, he had no name or story when he was rescued at the border. He had been abused, was malnourished, and was on the verge of death when he was rescued just before being sold over the border. They decided to name this young boy Lamar Alix Marlow after Lamar, who was so pivotal to seeing this community of rescue become a reality; Jean Alix Paul, who is our local Haitian partner and oversees the entire village; and, well . . . me. I just write and share stories!

It was a small sign that God, in his never-ending pursuit of making right what is wrong, will use people like us to get the job done. I played a role, as did Lamar and Pastor Jean Alix. But it could not have happened except for the hundreds of people like you who had joined the movement and played a crucial role!

# A Rescue Movement

A movement of rescue had started and hundreds of people were involved. When we decided to move forward after talking to the mayor, I knew we needed to raise a few hundred thousand dollars to build the community impact center. We needed homes, water projects, a kitchen and dining hall, a garden, the great wall of Haiti (for protection), and of course we would need to hire and train staff.

We put each of these projects on our Garage Sale for Orphans website, we told the story as best we could, and we asked our friends to throw garage sale parties. Friends posted the information on their blogs to help spread the word.

And just like that, churches, small groups, and families joined our dance, bringing $1,000, $12,000, $200—over and over. After a few months we had enough money to break ground. More people threw garage sale parties, and we began to build the homes.

Over 80 percent of all the funds that were raised to build the village were raised through garage sale money. Our tagline was simple: your excess can mean life for another. As kids were rescued, people—individuals, families, small groups—would then sponsor the children to provide the day-to-day needs and long-term sustainability for the kids and community.

If you were to walk into this village, you would be swarmed by kids running up to you to give you a hug. They have these big smiles and this joy that seems otherworldly. These kids were on the road to hell, but now, because of everyday, normal people who decided to be part of a larger movement, people who believe that doing good could be simple and significant, these kids have hope and a bright future.

What if doing good was simple? This is what we mean. It is not always easy; it does not mean we do not sacrifice. It usually requires hard work.

This is more than slacktivism, when you care more about other people knowing you care than about the cause itself. It's easy to use the story of the poor to build your own platform and make yourself feel good even if you did nothing to actually help.

I think we're all familiar with the Ice Bucket Challenge that went viral in 2014. Within a matter of days, people were pouring ice-cold water on their heads. Some did this because they care about ALS; others did this because they wanted to be seen on Facebook. Ultimately, we can all learn a lesson. The heartbreak of ALS was once again in our hearts and minds, and millions of dollars were raised. It was a simple yet powerful way to help. Even my daughter and her friends got involved.

My daughter did it because everyone else was doing it, but in her heart, she was also happy to be involved in something that mattered, something that was helpful.

Slacktivisim is a heart issue. A slacktivist is a person who is always talking but never doing—always hashtagging, never really helping. An activist is always trying to find small and big ways to help. Sometimes it is writing a check. Other times it is pouring ice water on your head. We get to choose who we want to be.

Simply put—we can all make a difference in the world. We can all make decisions that matter, that change the future, that create a better world. And yet, we don't carry a weight that is impossible. I can't solve all the issues of human trafficking in Haiti, much less the world, even though I wish I could. But I can be a part of a movement to fight trafficking in one community.

## We Can't Fix Everything Today!

When we hear stories about human trafficking or the global orphan crisis, it can all seem extremely overwhelming. I get that; I've been there. Over the years I've learned a lesson: overwhelmed people quit!

I have quit far too many times in my life. I've even experienced heartbreaking failures. Often I look back and wish I had not given up.

Over the past half decade, I've seen many people who care deeply for the poor, but they only last for a short season. It is like they were running a sprint without realizing they signed up for a marathon.

Those who run marathons slow down, focus, and concentrate on pace and consuming energy. They don't want to get injured, and fueling their bodies at the right time is vital for them to reach the finish line. They are not overemotional; calm wins the day. They know they have a fight on their hands and they need to pace themselves. Even more, the key to success is how they prepare during the months before race day!

As you join this movement of doing good, you need to prepare, you need endurance, you need focus, and most importantly, you need to pace yourself for the long run. It will be a challenge; you don't know how your body is going to react, you don't know how the weather will be. Uncertainty is everywhere. You will have to take risks, make decisions on the fly, and endure plenty of setbacks.

Just like marathoners, you have to come to grips with the fact that you cannot fix the entire world by daybreak. It is not going to happen. Don't be the person who loves hard and goes so fast that you run out of gas, give up, and ignore the calling to do good with your life.

When we start to run out of gas, it's not because we don't care; it is because we started to sprint instead of taking small but important ministeps forward. These steps are significant, helping us pace ourselves for the long haul ahead.

## Thin Place for Movement Makers

Have you ever heard the idea of a thin place? According to Celtic spiritual tradition, it is a place where the boundary between heaven and earth is especially thin. It's a place where we can sense the divine more readily.

One way to experience the thin place is to do good by loving your neighbor, stopping along the way, helping the wounded and broken, and caring for the fatherless, the widow, the slave. The thin place is the most important place in the world; it's a place for doers, folks who are involved in a movement of good and who live in the thick of mission.

God is close to his people when they are living out their calling. We can feel heaven breathing life on earth, and it fixes the brokenhearted, restores hope, and gives meaning to all—the rich, the poor and everyone in between. When we live in the thin place, we're all just a group of people who are loved by God and who love one another.

I know we all want to have meaning in our lives; we all ache to sense the closeness of God and to live on mission. When heaven and earth intermingle with one another and we are caught up in the middle? Those are goose-bump moments, sacred opportunities that ignite movements that do good in our heart and world.

But there is a downside to having an explosive emotional experience. We can't continue to live on this emotional high forever; it is only a matter of time until reality calls us back and emotions fade into the background and slowly disappear from our consciousness.

In this moment a decision must be made. A thin space will be required for long-term engagement. You cannot do this alone; you cannot do this in your own wisdom, strength, or power. There's a reason why Jesus sent a helper—the Holy Spirit—who is leading this do-good movement. When we forget that, we are on the road to burnout because we chose to carry the burdens of the world on our shoulders. But Jesus took that responsibility from us!

We must come to grips with reality and decide to pace ourselves for the long run ahead of us, knowing that at the end of the race we come face-to-face with our Maker, the leader of the movement, and that maybe, just maybe, we will hear those beautiful and epic words "well done." Because we danced, the work became more beautiful.

## A Story Worth More Than $.25

In 2010 I was traveling to a small, very rural village in Haiti. When you drive down the dusty back roads of Haiti, you pass young kids running around, clothed in only their smiles, free and with no concerns at all. Transportation in this community is mostly donkeys. If you are in the upper class, you might have a motorbike. Only occasionally did we see a car drive by.

On our journey to this part of Haiti, we traveled parallel to a river that looked more like chocolate milk than water. Yet this river was the water supply for the entire region. I was flabbergasted to see the locals using their buckets and collecting this water for cooking and drinking. Bathrooms in homes don't really exist in this community, so this river was also where the locals bathed. Sadly, this river became the breeding ground for cholera. Thousands of Haitians died, and this particular community was greatly affected.

As our van finally came to a stop and the dust settled, we were relieved to reach our final destination after hours of travel. The van had parked in front of the local medical clinic, and when I got out of the van, I peered through the iron gate. There were dozens of black body bags filled with men, women, and children who had lost their struggle against the monster known as cholera.

Though I didn't realize it at the time, this community would teach me more about poverty alleviation and movement making and doing good and doing it well than any textbook, article, seminar, or class ever could. Furthermore, it would demonstrate why wisdom is necessary as we approach such a complex subject.

After spending a few moments with the head doctor who runs the clinic, we walked down that dusty road and arrived at the school. This school is a beacon of hope in the middle of all this despair; it offers a chance to dream and believe in a better future.

Before we entered the school, Jean Alix introduced me to some of the local businessmen—all rice farmers—who had come to meet us. One glance in their eyes and you could see the weight they were carrying; it was too much.

After the earthquake, the world flooded Haiti with free rice. It was rice that was subsidized by foreign governments and handed out, free of charge, to the masses.

The US decided to send aid to Haiti. They used that aid money to buy rice from domestic farmers. Of course, it was a great way to stimulate the American economy. The rice was then shipped to Haiti and passed out for free. Of course, you know where I'm going: free always kills the market and closes down businesses. If you can get free rice, why pay?

In an emergency, this practice is acceptable so people do not starve. But ten months after the emergency, this practice becomes harmful and creates more suffering. The Haitian farmers had plenty of rice; it was everywhere. But no one would buy it from them, so they were broke, with few opportunities; sadly, plan Bs rarely exist in the developing world.

# Children in Black

When cholera exploded out of nowhere, it caught this community, the NGOs (non-government organizations), and the entire nation of Haiti off guard. There were no jobs, no clean water, and lots of death. To say that this community was struggling is an understatement. After we talked to the local business leaders, we made our way to the school. Usually when you visit a school, you see kids playing, smiling, and laughing. There is lots of noise and energy!

But that was not the case at this school. Thick depression and hopelessness hung over the community like a cloud attached to the Great Smoky Mountains. Many—too many—kids were dressed in black. I was told they were mourning the loss of a loved one who had died from cholera.

The principal began to point out students. This girl lost her sister and aunt, that boy lost his father and cousin. The principal was telling me their stories; there was so much suffering it was hard to bear. I just wanted to make it all stop.

And then we heard a crash; a commotion took place in the back of the room.

A young girl had fainted. She was roughly ten years old, thin and frail. My Haitian friends kneeled down to talk to her.

Eventually she regained her strength, sat up, and shared her story. As she talked, tears ran down her cheeks and her body shook. Her suffering was so real; my heart was breaking into a thousand pieces. Life is so unfair, but the tragedy of her life was far too normal for the region.

Because the community could no longer sell rice and it was hours away from any outside aid, families began to feed their children in shifts, as in only one child would get to eat that day. The principal told me that her family, like many in the community, could only feed their kids every other day, just to keep them alive.

This precious girl, one of God's beloved children, had not eaten in two days. Her hunger made her weak, but even worse was her thirst. That morning she walked to school—almost a full mile in the Haitian heat. Haiti is hot, and this community may be the hottest of the hot. It is flat, with few trees to provide shade. The sun pounds you in ways that seem unfair and unbearable. Of course, Haitians are mostly used to this kind of heat; the problem was that they had no access to water, no way to hydrate. This girl, like so many of her neighbors, refused to drink from the river. She was scared that she would die just like the others in the village.

Even after her collapse, after everything that she had been through that day, that week, that year, her entire life, her desperate need to learn still gripped her.

"I have to go to school. *Education is my only hope!*"

I will never forget those words.

# Got a Quarter?

We left the classroom, and I gathered with Jean Alix, the principal of the school, and Pastor Wilson, a local Haitian pastor. We all needed a second to compose ourselves, to whisper a silent prayer, or better yet, question God's love for humanity.

Sometimes, the suffering is just too much. I have to find my thin place.

I do not have a framework to understand the depth of this suffering. My kids have only known life with three meals a day and snacks whenever they desire. I want every kid to have the same luxury as mine.

You quickly realize that God's love for humanity is his people living for others, doing good, and sacrificing for each other. It is true, and it is biblical; John tells us that we are sent into the world (John 17:18). We must capture the importance of doing good and doing it well. Real lives are on the line, real lives are in need of help, and real lives can be transformed by our generosity!

This is about a girl in a village who is suffering. She, and children like her everywhere, needs to see the hands and feet of God—his people—come through to relieve her suffering, allow hope to live in her heart, and help her thrive and flourish. Justice is real; it has skin on it and requires a lot. But guess what—it can be so simple!

You and I have *more* than most. We can make an impact; it can be simple, yet it can change the world of one little child. Hope is always searching for a way to be unleashed, and it is freed when we choose to be a people of love, service, and sacrifice.

Before we go forward, let's go back to that rural village. The story is not over yet.

I asked a simple question to my Haitian friends. "How much does it cost to feed these kids a meal?" The three of them—the principal, Jean Alix, and Pastor Wilson—huddled together and discussed the math. They have fed thousands of people over decades; they're experts. They know this work, they know the cost, and they know the impact.

After a minute or so, Jean Alix looked me in the eye and said, "About 25 cents, per kid, per meal."

Twenty-five cents. Now that sounds like a movement waiting to happen.

## Doing Good, a Bag of Coffee at a Time

My friend Joe is the owner of Raleigh Coffee Company, and he loves to find ways to use his passion and business to do good. He has truly found his thin place in life. I told Joe about Drouin, and immediately I could see his mind churning. Joe is a normal guy with a wife and two young kids; he is also an owner trying to run a profitable business. But he wants to make an impact in the world, so he thought of a simple way to do just that: every time he sells a bag of coffee, he donates $.25 to Drouin so a child can be fed. And he's inviting others to do the same.

Joe's coffee company is starting a movement of coffee drinkers who are creating an impact and ensuring that young girls don't pass out in class. It's small, it's simple, but it is important work that matters. Movements can be massive, like the ice bucket challenge; movements can be world-shifting, like the Egyptian uprising; or movements can be as simple as a coffee business owner who is helping keep families together by doing what he loves and being generous in the process.

## Making a Difference Long Term

When God strikes your heart with passion and compassion, when you join the movement of justice seekers—ordinary, everyday warriors who are on a mission to do good and do it well—you have to begin to make a long-term plan of action. That plan must begin with knowing your roles, responsibilities, and the tools you have to fight with.

Let me use my story to maybe help you discover your story.

I feel that we have a twofold role: As disciples of Jesus we are called to bring the good news of the gospel to our world. We are called to love, share the story of Christ, and how it has impacted our lives. We are also called to serve and do good. When we mix up our roles, we get sideways quickly.

My calling, vocationally, is to lead Help One Now. This is what I focus on each day. For you, your primary calling may be to run a business, work in a law firm, take care of the kids at home, crunch numbers, work at a church, fight fires, create laws, balance budgets, or run a start-up company. *All work matters.*

The reason why so many folks experience that thin place, the sacred moments and the deep connection, and then eventually ignore what they felt is because they forgot what they are called to do and how they are called to do it and at what level they are called to engage. They are taking on the weight of too many issues. Don't do that; you are not a superhero. We are all humans and can only bear so much.

My vocation is to serve the poor and give people like you tools with which you can also serve the poor, knowing that you also have to work and focus on other vital responsibilities in life. Our roles are vastly different; you can't be me and I can't be you. We have different functions and callings and outcomes, but we are both part of this great movement to do good!

And this is when it gets really fun and exciting—imagine if we never burnt out. What if we came back from having a thin-place moment and we were able to make a long-term impact?

We started to pace ourselves for the long journey, knowing along the way that we're going to make a significant difference in the world. We know our roles and have a clear understanding of how to engage.

We are not sprinting, trying to change all the brokenness overnight; instead, we are prepared for a lifetime of focus and are fully committed to doing good and walking in the freedom of knowing that we have a helper who is carrying the load and leading the way.

This leads me to my next point.

*Realize that you do not have to fix everything.*

You can't; that is not your problem or role. Take a moment, breathe, and allow that truth to bring peace to your weary soul.

The more I do the kind of work I do, the more I realize how important embracing this truth truly is.

God tells us that his burden is easy and his yoke is light. You see, when you experience the thin space, you look into that mirror and you see the divine, the One who has never-ending strength and wisdom and power. You see the One who will someday fix all of this. Tears will dry up and disappear, mourning will give way to worship, joy will explode, and all will be well and whole again.

Oh, how I long for that day to arrive. . . .

## Waiting for Heaven, Fighting Hell's Fury

Until then, we have a calling to live out, a role to play, a Helper to guide us forward. He will use our gifts, resources, and talents to do good and make a difference, to love, sacrifice, and fight. With God leading the way, I can run the race long-term and not be overwhelmed. I can enjoy the day-to-day rhythms of life; I can have fun during the day and go to bed in the tent-cities of Haiti.

Some days I will mourn over the pain of the world, and at other times I will be filled with joy when I see how good is overcoming evil. This is the race: one step forward, one day at a time!

But no matter what is taking place, I know that I don't have to fix everything. This is why we named our organization Help One Now. You and I can help one person, we can sponsor one child, we can commit to serving one community. Less is more; narrow your focus, dig deeper, and feel the joy of clarity and keeping life simple.

So go ahead and cast all of your burdens on him—right now! Be prepared to run the race for the remainder of your life, and be a part of a movement shaping a new and better world.

# 8

# Better Together

## *How to Find a Good Organization and Partner Together*

[Love] is a language to be learned, a musical
instrument to be practiced, a mountain to be
climbed via some steep and tricky cliff paths
but with the most amazing view from the top.

N. T. Wright

Back in 2010, when we were a baby organization that could barely afford to pay our bills or help kids around the world, I had a meeting with a new friend Barclay. I shared my heart and the vision of Help One Now. Barclay immediately got involved. He started to give monthly, took multiple trips with us, and started to advocate on our behalf.

Now, Barclay is not a wealthy retiree. In fact, he is a sales executive, and he is also the father of two boys. He has an extremely busy life, and yet he has been involved in our story ever since that day we met for lunch.

This is just one story of the hundreds of everyday people

who have been engaged in Help One Now for many years. It is because of the Barclays in the world that we can do what we do. It takes time, collaboration, and a commitment for the long haul.

So where do you start? How can you find your own long-term partnership?

Trying to get involved with any charitable organization can feel like an IKEA moment. You know what I mean—when I open a box, pull out the instructions, and look at the pictures, I just want to give up. You get one tool, hundreds of parts, and usually just two or three images that seem to be created by elementary kids on a sugar high.

Finding a good organization to partner with can be like this: overwhelmingly confusing. There are so many philosophies, so many options, so many opportunities. I want to help you gain clarity as you consider which organizations you want to partner with. I hope that you find nuggets of wisdom that will be beneficial as you take the next steps in doing good. By no means is it linear or all encompassing. But maybe a framework is starting to take shape so you can do good, do it well, and do it together. This is what it means to be connected to a movement of other people and organizations who are doing good.

## Collaboration Is Essential

Collaboration is powerful. When we choose to collaborate, we come to the table with all of our passions, network, intellect, gifts, and resources to tackle a problem together. For most of us, extreme poverty will be something we tackle as a calling and passion but not as a vocation.

For those of us who make our living by working with organizations that are fighting poverty, we have the time and mental capacity to lean deep into these issues. We can focus, study, and research as we try to grasp the problems and find solutions. Then we can give you tools, stories, data, and opportunity to help solve the problem and make progress.

This is how we can collaborate together and do good. I believe the best way for you to help, for you to make a tangible impact, is to partner with key organizations that you love and trust. Yet you must have a very clear vision of your role and goals; you are too busy and the problems too real for you to lack clarity.

Often one way that we can really make an impact is to understand the power of our networks. We run in tribes of like-minded people who are connected by similar passions. Take a moment and think about your friends, family, coworkers, and neighbors. Maybe you will quickly realize that your network has a lot of potential to do good. Maybe what they need is a guide like you to help them unlock their human capital and engage. Maybe they could give money, maybe they could give a talent, or maybe they could give their voice and advocate. This is a powerful way to make an impact in the world.

# How to Partner Well

So, here's a simple guide that will help you process how to find a good organization, what to expect, and how to collaborate well.

## 1. Do Something Rather Than Nothing

Committing your mind to action creates a certain ethos in who you are and who you will become. Commit to being a doer of the Word; do something, and that something, though it may seem small and insignificant in the beginning, will lead to another action step, and then another. Momentum will take over, and all of sudden you will see an avalanche of good rolling down the mountain; as the prophet Amos says, "Let justice roll on like a river, righteousness like a never-failing stream!" (Amos 5:24).

When you commit to doing something rather than nothing, you are telling yourself and the world that you are choosing to live an action-oriented life rather than a passive-oriented life. You become part of a movement that is dancing together.

## 2. Start Small

Remember, you're not trying to change the world overnight. This is a marathon; the goal is to take one step at a time. When I get frustrated, overwhelmed, or feel like giving up, I just remind myself that a "win" sometimes comes inch by inch.

I would encourage you to pray; ask God for direction, wisdom, and clarity. Then, make one commitment that will make a difference. That could be advocating for an organization or cause or writing your very first check—even a very small check. It does not have to be massive to make a massive impact; everything matters. Doing good can scale as you drill down, create an action plan, and get comfortable in your role.

Starting small could be something as simple as rearranging your budget to give you the wiggle room to be more generous. Have a talk with your family and friends to let them know the plan and why you're passionate about helping. If your entire family or friend group is involved, it is a great opportunity to connect on a deeper level, disciple your kids, and teach them about love, service, compassion, and beauty.

Doing good will become a natural part of your life. Little by little, you will see it seep into everything, like how you use your time, how you spend your money, and which people you choose to do life with. Again, this is a simple but very significant step in your search for purpose, meaning, and personal calling.

### 3. Follow Your Passions

Ask yourself, "What am I passionate about? What makes my blood boil?" That will help you focus on organizations that are doing work within the area that you love.

Another way to find your passion is to find what inspires you. I have some friends who are inspired by travel; they will go anywhere and do anything. Other friends love strategy—they will sit and whiteboard all day long—while other friends love to advocate and amplify our work.

What do you love to do? What makes you angry? What

inspires you to work hard? What steals your sleep? If you can connect your passions to an organization that is helping to solve like-minded problems, magic can happen and collaboration becomes natural and powerful.

Doing good, while it may be hard and complex, can still be simple when you love to do it—when you feel like you were created to do the work and solve the problem.

## 4. Use Your Gifts

We need you. I simply cannot overstate this. I want to write an entire chapter that is filled with those words, over and over. *We need you!* Those who are suffering in extreme poverty need you. You were created with powerful gifts; those gifts were given so you could fight evil with good and do work that matters, that is vital, that is unique.

- If you are a writer, please use that gift to pen stories that create change.
- If you are a financial guru, please offer your talent to an organization that is in need of help.
- If you thrive in hospitality, volunteer and help create moments that matter.
- If you love to give money, please write checks with joy.
- If you have a small or big network, use that network to do good. You have the gift of influence; leverage it.
- If you are a speaker, use your stage to advocate for the poor and for organizations who are working on solving problems.

- If you are a strategist, use your gift to help an organization be organized, effective, and efficient.
- If you are a photographer, your pictures can capture the beauty and pain and can tell a story and cause people to take action.

I could go on and on; there are so many gifts, and they are all needed. Help One Now could never have succeeded without the talents, passions, and gifts of our tribe. We did not succeed because of one person; thousands came together, used their gifts, and created a movement of doing good.

## 5. Build Relationships

In the last decade, we've seen a huge shift. Folks want to be more involved; they want to get dirty. Many are not writing checks just to get a tax write-off; they are writing checks because they deeply care about an issue and they want to solve a problem.

This is beautiful; we have seen this with Help One Now. Many in our tribe are connected to doing good because of a relationship. We're doing this together; we are connected, we are involved, we are a tribe. A tribe needs a leader, and a leader needs a tribe; together, that leader and tribe can change the world and solve real problems.

This is why we need you to use your gifts but also to feel a sense of connectedness to the story. You can write checks and send them in the mail or donate online, and that is awesome (and *thank you*). But life change happens when we're together, doing good, using our gifts, and connecting to one another. This creates powerful opportunity for a true, long-lasting movement.

## 6. Stick with It

The journey is long, the mountain is high, the problems are real, and we won't solve them overnight. We are not sprinting but running a marathon—heck, maybe an Ironman. When we get to the finish line, the feeling will be amazing. The work and sacrifice will pay off and you will get to see how God used everyday people like you and me to make a difference—to do good, do it well, and do it together.

But you have to stay the course. You will need to do some research and then choose organizations to support. As a rule, I would encourage you to just pick one local and one global (I'm assuming you're also involved in your local church) and then add a time commitment.

For example, commit to these two organizations for the next two years. Join their tribe; go all in, be committed. Even when it is hard—be committed. It is so worth it.

How do you find this organization? Usually you will have a family member or good friend who is helping an organization; start there first. Ask yourself a series of questions to make sure you are connecting with an organization that fits your values, convictions, and passions.

Research the organization. Visit its website, study its finances, and get comfortable. Learn more about the organization's leadership; try to have a quick phone call or meeting so you understand their vision. Follow the stories they are telling through social media, their newsletter, or their blog.

Of course, you can also find formal data online: Charity Navigator, ECFA, and GuideStar are all great resources. While these sites are not perfect, they will give you a sense of direction and key data.

Think about these questions:

- Are they trustworthy?
- Do the projects they talk about actually happen?
- Are they making a real, tangible impact?
- Are they empowering the people and countries in which they serve?
- Do they have an engaged and excited donor base?
- Are they innovating?
- Are they giving the donor tools to use to help and advocate on their behalf?
- Are they financially transparent?
- Are they thoughtful and humble in how they approach their work?

## Progress, Inch by Inch

One of my favorite stories is from *Great by Choice*, a business book by Jim Collins. Collins shares about two explorers, Amundsen and Scott, who were both on a mission to be the first explorers to reach the South Pole.

The trek was roughly the distance from New York to Chicago and in treacherous conditions. Temperatures could reach twenty degrees below zero, even in the summer months.

They both led teams, but they had very different tactical philosophies. Before any journey started, Amundsen prepared rigorously for the journey and any obstacles that his team would face. This was not the case for Scott, who decided his intuition was more vital than real data and preparation.

Once the trek started, these two explorers had vastly different work ethics. Scott was chaotic, always changing based on current conditions. For instance, one day they would trek two miles, the next day they would not leave their base camp because of the frigid cold, and then they would try to go full blast for days on end just to catch up. This led to exhaustion.

Amundsen's team, no matter the conditions, always marched anywhere from 12–20 miles a day, without fail. Every day they made progress and used their energy properly. The team knew that no matter what, they were moving forward and making progress, and they were confident they had the proper supplies for the trek.

On December 15, 1911, Amundsen's team reached the South Pole. A month later, Scott's team also made it there, where a Norwegian flag that the Amundsen team had placed greeted them. Sadly, running low on supplies, energy, and time, Scott's team never made it back to base camp. They all died just ten miles short of their supply depot.

Remember we discussed that we're running a marathon, not a sprint, so are we preparing for a long, hard journey. We want to make it back alive, we want to see progress, we want to do good and do it well, and we want to see the good news of the gospel living in the tangible.

No doubt we would all agree that we now live in a world full of distractions. There are more than enough opportunities, far too many needs, and not enough time and resources for us to be involved in all of them. Amundsen's exploration is paralleled in Scripture, where we see biblical heroes who also embraced the reality that their callings were not sprints but long, hard-fought journeys to do good.

- Abraham was called to leave his country and go to the place God would show him—to start the long journey to the promised land.
- Moses was called to help lead people from the slave fields of Egypt into the promised land.
- Jesus was born a baby, worked as a carpenter, and then one day at a wedding party, he knew it was time. He began a long, painful march that ended on a hill called Golgotha.
- The apostle Paul always had his eyes set on Rome, but it took him multiple missionary journeys until he finally arrived.
- Hebrews 11 talks about all the amazing men and women of God—heaven's hall of fame, if you will. Hebrews 12 starts with a simple reminder of what these folks did; they removed all hindrances and ran a race with perseverance until the end.

- Paul instructed the Corinthians not to run aimlessly, but rather to have a goal and a focus (1 Corinthians 9:26–27).

Doing good requires long-term thinking and planning. If done right, it will be like saving for your retirement; you will create a rhythm of doing good that feels natural and yes, sacrificial, but it won't be aimless. Rather, it will have a sense of focus mixed with preparation and faith.

## What Does This Look Like?

Help One Now has many different ways to get involved and many unique people who make up our tribe. Many have been trekking with us since day one; others have just joined the journey and we hope they stick around for decades.

I remember speaking at Austin New Church. This was the first time I had spoken in a public setting about my experience in Zimbabwe. I cried a lot. Jen was on the front row; she cried a lot as well. Brandon is also known to cry from time to time (read: all the time).

I asked them to help me launch this organization. At the time, we had nothing but a story from a gas station and a lot of passion! But we were bonded by this desire to see the church lead the fight on issues of justice.

Austin New Church got involved, and Jen and Brandon personally got involved. Together we have fought to make the world brighter. Jen joined our board (which means she can totally fire me—I love you, Jen!); together we have traveled around the world, met with our leaders, told stories of love and hope, and asked people to jump on board and help.

Six years later, we are all still moving forward. I could have never done this without them. They had much better opportunities with other organizations that have more clout. But they took a risk and have stayed the course and helped push us forward. This matters!

A small church in downtown Austin, New City Austin, did the same thing. My friend Jacob was on our first trip to Haiti, and his eighty-member church wrote the largest check that we had received up to that point to help care for Pastor Gaetan's kids. When I drove to the bank to deposit the check, I thought for sure that it would bounce. This was 2010; most churches were holding on to their cash, yet this small church invested in us and the kids in Haiti right when they were living under a tree and needed help the most. This eighty-member church plant literally launched all of our work in Haiti; they were pioneers.

Six years later, they're still walking side by side with us. Together, we do our best to journey forward constantly, and year after year we see the fruit of our collaborative labor. A tribe is able to share life and stories with one another, and their collective impact is far greater than if one person were doing all the work.

There's also this community in northwest Arkansas. After the earthquake in Haiti, they asked me to come share and then ended up being the ones who bought many of the T-shirts after the Haitian earthquake. This community of friends has been fighting with us to make the world better. They have experienced all the ups and all the downs. Without these folks, I doubt Help One Now would even exist.

These are just a few examples of what it means to trek together for the long haul, to do work that matters, and to go through ups and downs, experience wins and losses, enjoy moments that have meaning—like the time over *four hundred*! kids were sponsored on our Love Hope trip to Ethiopia, and we celebrated like crazy people together in the airport. Or when Sarah Bessey, who had helped build the school in Haiti, was able to come back and visit— that moment when, seeing what she helped to do, tears of humble joy streamed down her cheeks. These are sacred moments—the big payoffs to the hard work, struggle, and sacrifice.

## Created to Create Beauty

We're called, as God's people, to create beauty together. In my mind, I hear the sound of the waves crashing against the beach on the Carolina coast. I see and hear the beauty that is God's creation. I can just stare for days and do nothing. God created a beautiful world, but sin wants to take that beauty and make it ugly.

Thankfully, there's the church, whom God has called to take the ugly and broken parts of the world and make them beautiful again. I find it amazing that God, who created the heavens and earth, who is the King of *all* kings and the Lord of *all* lords, invites broken people like you and me to help repair the world.

As we dance together, we soon realize that God is the one who has started the music.

I hope this will fill your soul with meaning, purpose, and clarity. I think this is what it means to live a life of abundance. We are the workers and we have to get to work, doing good and seeing the ugly become beautiful again. When God and his people walk together, powerful stories come to life; some are small, some are big, but they all matter.

Imagine what the rest of the world would think of Christians if we fought hard for those who suffer, if ordinary people like us lived a life that is in fact not ordinary at all. We can love deeper, give more, serve together, and feel a sense of mission. We belong to God, we belong to one another, and each day we do our best to capture the opportunities right in front of us.

The kingdom of God will be found when we choose to leave the comforts of the Christian subculture and experience the joy of life in the middle of the world's mess and sin and devastation. It may not look clean and tidy. We may not have nice, pat answers to all the world's questions, but what we will have is far greater—a story about a God who was willing to lay his life down, and stories about his people who are also willing to lay their lives down.

When people ask why I am doing all of this good, I want to say it is because I serve a God who is good!

Together, our little, imperfect tribe is doing what we can with our passions, talents, and resources. Like Amundsen, who marched twenty miles a day for the entire journey, we are committed to working daily to help write a better ending to an epic story of creation. We have all experienced the ramifications of the fall; no doubt sin destroys, but redemption is living, and we want to be a part of that redemptive story.

What a joy and privilege it is to make the ugly, beautiful. This is why we keep marching!

## Dig Deep, but Change If Needed

Please hear me out; what I'm not saying is that you just made a lifetime commitment when you chose an organization. Change is natural; it happens and that is okay. What I am saying is this: be ready to commit and dig deep, but that does not mean you won't pivot or change directions.

If you realize the organization you are committed to is not doing good work, change. If you feel disconnected and not cared for or appreciated (and you have proper expectations), change.

If you have an amazing opportunity with another organization, take a step back, pray and process, and then change if need be.

## When My Friend Stopped Sponsoring a Child

I have a good friend named Bill who leads a great nonprofit in Guatemala. I have another good friend named Todd who is a bearded Portland hipster. Todd and his church partnered with Help One Now in the early days.

Todd adopted a boy from Guatemala and wanted to give back to that country. The three of us just happened to be speaking at a conference on justice, the Idea Camp. I introduced Todd to my friend Bill, and they hit it off since they both had a deep passion for the people of Guatemala.

Todd called me a few weeks later and shared his heart. I had spoken at his church, we were processing partnership, and Todd and his family sponsored a child with Help One Now. But we don't work in Guatemala. So Todd asked me if it was cool for his family to pivot and get involved in Lemonade International.

Of course it was okay. Todd had a clear line of sight. He knew he was called to serve the people of Guatemala, and as a friend, I knew his heart (and Bill's heart) were in the right place. Eventually Todd's church partnered with Lemonade and Todd was invited on their board. Together they have made a true impact.

Bill, Todd, and I are good friends. And I believe that better work is being done because of those decisions. It's okay to be flexible and change. I would just encourage you to do your best not always to be in a constant cycle of change. This is like the church hoppers; they are never satisfied. As soon as one thing goes wrong, they are off searching for a new church. These kinds of folks rarely, if ever, make a lasting impact because they are not around long enough to form deep roots.

Change can be good and healthy, and it can lead to a clearer focus and greater impact. Todd has been a wonderful advocate for Help One Now. He loves our work, but he is laser focused and able to put all of his time, energy, and resources to serving the good people of Guatemala, which means the kingdom of God is the biggest benefactor.

Hopefully you now have practical steps to engage, you are fully committed to the twenty-mile march, and you're also ready to pivot if needed. My hope is that this practical information will help you do good and do it well so you can experience the beauty of the journey and see the impact your life can have.

# Conclusion:
# As Good as It Gets

*For my yoke is easy, and my burden is light.*
**Jesus**

By the time this book is published, it will be close to ten years from the time I encountered the unknown orphan at the abandoned gas station in Zimbabwe. Not long ago, I was back in Zimbabwe visiting my friends and partners.

The kids are getting older now. They are starting to look like young adults. They remind me of my kids. I mourn their growing up; I wish I was able to spend more time with them.

Many of the kids are no longer there. They have been reunited with their families or have come of age. Our next step is to create a world-class transition program so these kids will become the next generation of leaders in Zimbabwe.

Going back is always a sacred experience for me. It is like walking on holy ground—the thinnest of thin places. I'm reminded of God's great grace and mercy. He was patient with me back then and still is today. We have seen amazing progress, we have made a million mistakes, and we're still trying to answer some hard questions for the future of these kids.

I was told by Elizabeth, who runs the day-to-day operations at the children's home, that the Zimbabwe government uses our model as an example to others who desire to start new children's homes.

Imagine that! Somehow we have created a model that is recognized by the government as effective, a model worthy to be copied. Of course by now, when I say "we," I hope you know what I mean.

It is because of our local leaders, John and Orpha, and my friends, Steven and Amy. They blazed a trail and created a pathway on which our amazing tribe—those who sponsored kids, threw garage sale parties, and donated to Christmas campaigns— could walk.

They are everyday heroes who are doing what they can to make an impact in the world.

I'm still amazed that we've been able to play a small role and see real transformation. Thousands of people are involved in our story; they have been able to capture what true meaning and purpose is like. They are Good Samaritans who stopped along the way to help a group of orphans in Zimbabwe as well as others around the world. I've had hundreds of conversations, and I think we would all agree that, just like giving is far better than receiving, loving your neighbor is not only good for your neighbor, it is also good for you because you and I were created to do good.

We have come so far, and we still have a long way to go. But we have made progress!

# Living in the Broken Places

I have no doubt that doing good will often bring tears of sadness to your cheeks as you come face to face with hell's fury. But tears of joy will come when it seems as if heaven did visit earth and somehow you got to experience it. Doing good will bring freedom to your soul. You find this place of peace, rest, and comfort that does not really make a lot of sense.

You become comfortable living in the broken spaces of humanity.

Perhaps this will scare some of you. But when you read in Scripture that his yoke is easy and his burden is light (Matthew 11:30), and then you read that you should lay down your life (1 John 3:16), how do you make sense of that?

It depends on how you see the world working. For me, I have come to a place of peace that God reigns in my soul and I share in this mission, but I'm also able to cast my cares on him. I am able to remove the burdens of extreme poverty, and I'm able to be at peace with the evil that exists in our world.

I think what happens is that you mature as you continue to march forward; you realize while you are marching that you don't have the weight of the world on your shoulders. You do not have to live with anxiety because you can't solve all the world's problems.

I desperately want to see you run the race. We need you because you matter. I'm praying for workers. I also want to see you cross the finish line. I imagine this will be a place of joy and reflection, a chance to look back and see the tension between the complex and simple, the hard and easy.

I feel as if we will truly be able to say that doing good was in fact simple—not easy, but simple. Because all along we were just following the way of Jesus, and all along he has given us what we have needed to do good and do it well.

## A New World Is Possible

We have a world to change, we have work to do, we have progress to make, we have real lives who need us to care, love, and give—not just for a day, a month, or a year, but for the remainder of our days.

Sometimes it's difficult to have grace for those who may not be as passionate as you are about a certain cause. People often can't see what you and I can see; they don't believe the world can get better, that hope is rising, that men and women can find deep purpose and meaning when we choose to love and do good.

I remember sitting in a coffee shop in Austin in 2008, a few months after my first trip to Zimbabwe. I had placed a sticker on my computer that said something like: "Poverty sucks; let's end it."

Out of nowhere, a man walked up to me, pointed to the sticker, and asked me about it. I told him why I have it on the computer, about my trip to South Africa and Zimbabwe, and the current global orphan crisis. He replied with a smart-aleck remark: "We will never end poverty, and those people are getting what they deserve."

My blood began to boil in silence for a moment. He left my

little table and went to his own on the other side of the room. By this time I was furious, so after I hyperventilated, whispered a few prayers such as: "God, can you please strike down that dude or at least make sure his coffee burns his tongue? Either one— judgment is in your hands!" I finally got out of my seat, walked up to the able, and I punched him in the face.

Just kidding. I just thought about it and decided that would not be rad. What I did do was sit down in the empty chair on the other side of his table. I gently shut his laptop, and he stared at me in panic as we made eye contact.

I asked him what he meant by his statement and asked if he had ever been to any country in Africa. Then I told him my story. He was speechless, mumbled a little bit of this and that, and then somewhat apologized. I have no clue if God answered my prayers and burned his tongue with that hot, scalding coffee, but probably not (thankfully, God is a bit nicer than I am).

I walked away and processed this encounter, and I realized that we can change the world, but we will have our trolls, skeptics, critics, and doubters. These are the people who choose to whine and complain and who will always be upset. They will despise you when you choose to live differently while they themselves have no desire to change.

Some of these people will be found on a stage every Sunday morning, sharing the so-called gospel that does not include justice. Others will be in your small groups. They love Jesus, but justice, now . . . that's a different kind of story.

Many of your family members might mock you as well. Your

social media "friends" will ask, "Why are you helping kids over there when we have needs right here in our own backyard?" All of these people will come out of the woodwork with flaming arrows ready to inflict pain and shame on anyone who is doing what they are too scared to do—care for people.

I used to get mad at these people, but now I just feel sad for them. I'm sad they have such little vision, sad they don't understand what it means to love and care deeply. Sad they think some imaginary border makes "us" better than "them," as if borders confine the Holy Spirit and God's church.

Now I pray for these folks, and I hope that someday they will experience this amazing calling to love so deeply that it hurts yet also causes us to live a life with such purpose and meaning. Grace wins! I needed grace and I found it, or maybe it found me. I really don't care; I just needed it, and I still do!

## We're Winning the Battle

In the last seven years, here is what I know. The world is changing. Extreme poverty has been cut in half;[1] malaria is being wiped off the face of the earth; new technologies have emerged and created powerful, innovative opportunities; hundreds of millions of people now have access to clean water and sanitation; and our approach to caring for the poor is changing from "we will fix it for them" to "we will fight the battle with them."

What a great time to be alive! We have so many opportunities to make a difference. Each day I talk to my friends from all over the world for free online. As little as eight years ago, that would have been impossible. But emerging technology has shrunk the global footprint and created an opportunity for deep connection, friendships, and collaboration.

As a whole, we should be thoroughly encouraged by the progress. Yet we should also be prepared for the next round in the battle.

I think we would all agree that the world is volatile. Terrorism, wars, diseases, natural disasters, climate change. There are so many countries caught in the crossfire. Often we take two steps forward and one step back; that is okay, as long as we keep moving.

I say this not to be negative; rather, I want you to wrestle with this deep sense of meaning and purpose and calling in your life. When it seems as if the world is crumbling around us and the problems are far too big for any of us, doing good has to be simple for the masses.

We need to narrow our focus, grow deep roots, and commit to the process without carrying the weight of the world on our shoulders. I hope you are running this race with me today. If not, it's your chance to start, right here and right now.

It is not because we don't care; it is actually because we care so much that we can't allow ourselves to run the race and not see the finish line. We pace ourselves, one step at a time, over and over. Many of you may feel a deeper calling to engage these issues as a vocation; that is awesome. For most of you, when you close this book, you will go change another diaper, head off to work once again, or maybe open a schoolbook and begin to study. But please know this—you are important! You are needed!

# Struggle for Progress

I was in Uganda touring a school. Our local leader had rescued a child, Olivia, from trafficking and reunited that child with her family. A few years later, she was thriving in school and had earned a place in a private school, which is a big deal in Uganda.

She was a teenager when we came back to visit. As we walked up to the gate of her school, we saw this saying wrought into the gate itself: *Struggle for Progress.*

I was with a group of longtime Help One Now advocates, team members, and board members—Lamar, Mike, Scotty, Adam, Brandon, Tim, and me. We just kind of froze. Those words sunk deep into our souls because this is what we are doing. If we are going to continue to help girls like Olivia, we're going to have to struggle for progress every single day.

Part of our struggle is to tell stories of hope, create tools for the masses to make a difference, and empower and resource our local leaders so we can care for kids and see their communities transformed.

One year later we were in a van in Ethiopia with a group of writers on our Love Hope trip. Our local leader, Aschalew, who leads Kidmia Ethiopia, had been doing some amazing work to help Ethiopian families adopt Ethiopian orphans. He wanted to expand his impact, so Kidmia asked if we would collaborate with them to do community development work.

This was our second time in Ethiopia with this giant of a leader. On this trip, we heard Aschalew say one thing over and over:

*"Together we build."*

# Together We Build

As I pen the final words of this book, I'm back in that same coffee shop where Ken, Jasen, and I first began to dream of living an others-focused life. That dream would eventually become Help One Now. After years of avoiding the call that I knew God placed on my heart to care for the poor, it took a fateful encounter with a young, unknown orphan in Zimbabwe to reignite the dreams birthed in those coffeehouse conversations in 2003.

The words on the school gate and the words of our local partner in Ethiopia have now become words the Help One Now tribe lives by.

We are changing the world; of that I have no doubt. I see it happening every day. God's people are seeing a kingdom that is much bigger and way more powerful than we ever imagined. At this point, we're all just trying to keep up with God, whom Psalms describes as a God of justice. He is on the move to make what is wrong, right. The ugly is becoming beautiful; the broken, healed. God is dancing.

His call to you is simple: join us in the struggle for progress, because together we are building a better world. A more Jesus-like world. It will not be easy. It will require sacrifice, but don't worry; Jesus' burden is light, his yoke is easy, and he has given you talents, gifts, resources, and passion.

Now, let's run the race as we learn to do good, seek justice, correct oppression, stand for the widow, and care for the fatherless!

You see, doing good *is* simple. And not only that, it is wildly significant.

Step by step. Moment by moment. Whether it's sponsoring a child, volunteering your Saturday, collecting spare change, or running a lemonade stand from your front yard. We struggle for progress. Together we build, trusting God is on the move.

# Acknowledgments

How does one thank the countless people who helped make this book a reality? It seems impossible!

I want to thank:

Jen Hatmaker, for encouraging me to write this book and share the stories of Help One Now while we were going through security in the Miami airport.

My agent, Christopher Ferebee, for giving me the confidence that this idea did not suck and for representing me well.

Jonathan Merritt, for your coaching and expertise, and for spending three days helping me shape the book into what it is today.

Stephanie Smith, the best editor in the world. I'm so thankful for your guidance and work. I could not have done this without you.

Ken Nussbaum, my editor before the editor, for helping me complete this project. You saved Stephanie tons of work and saved me tons of embarrassment. It was a long, hard journey, but we did it. (Yes, I needed an editor before the editor.)

Zondervan, for saying yes and believing in a rookie author who believes that we all can change the world.

Help One Now team and board (past, present, and future), our leaders around the world, and our tribe. This book is penned to honor you for your hard work and for the sacrifices you've made to bring hope to the world every day. You are brilliant, loving, filled with compassion, and tenacious. The best is yet to come and the world is better because of you!

My Friends who have shaped the journey:

Charles Lee, Mike and Corrie Rusch, Brandon and Jen Hatmaker, Jacob Vanhorn, Sarah Bessey, Willie and Korie Robertson, Adam and Stephanie Maass, Jacob and Emily Kaler, Scott and Mollie Paige, Bill and Cherie Cummings, Jasen and Amanda Ashdown, Keith Kall, Steve Graves, Seth and Amber Haines, Jason and Joy Standridge, Blaine and Gin Boyer, Kayla Glasgow, John Gilbert, Lindsey Strobel, the entire Pure Charity Team, Tre Wyatt, Scott and Tiffany Wade, Jeff and Christy Mangum, Lamar and Jill Stockton, John and Sherri Chandler, Sherry Birk, Kevin and Mollie Burpo, Joe and Katie Quartucci, Ken and Brenda Nussbaum, Payton and Heather Junkin, The IdeaCamp Tribe, and the Church on Morgan community.

BREW Coffee Bar in Raleigh, NC, for saving my seat to write every day and filling my cup with the best coffees from around world, via the Raleigh Coffee Company.

Necole, Bailey, and Mackenzie: thanks for being awesome, fun, and courageous as our little family has tried to do good and inspire others to do good, too. I know you made many sacrifices in the process, but together we have struggled for progress.

To that boy I met at that gas station. I remember your face, but sadly, I was never able to remember your name. I don't know how life turned out for you. I hope everything is okay. But I wanted to thank you for starting a movement of everyday, normal people who are committed to doing good by empowering leaders, caring for kids, and seeing communities transformed. I hope we get to dance together in heaven!

# Notes

## Introduction: Good Grief

1. United Nations, "Millennium Development Goals," *Resources for Speakers on Global Issues*, accessed December 11, 2015, http://www.un.org/en/globalissues/briefingpapers/mdgs/vitalstats.shtml.

## Chapter 1: Lemonade with a Purpose

1. United Nations, "Hunger," *Resources for Speakers on Global Issues*, accessed December 11, 2015, http://www.un.org/en/globalissues/briefingpapers/food/vitalstats.shtml.

2. Diana Garland, "Christian Families Serving Together: A Review of the Research," *Family and Community Ministries* 25 (2012): 45–67. Available online, http://www.faithformationlearningexchange.net/uploads/5/2/4/6/5246709/christian_families_serving_together.pdf

## Chapter 2: Ordinary Is the New Radical

1. Cited in Unesco, "The Slave Route," accessed December 14, 2015, http://www.unesco.org/new/en/culture/themes/dialogue/the-slave-route/resistances-and-abolitions/william-wilberforce/.

## Chapter 3: Despite Your Fears and Failures

1. Brennan Manning, *Ruthless Trust: The Ragamuffin's Path to God* (New York: HarperCollins, 2009), 5.


## Chapter 6: Good and Plenty

1. Erwin McManus, *Seizing Your Divine Moment: Dare to Live a Life of Adventure* (Nashville: Thomas Nelson, 2002), 50.


## Chapter 7: All Great Things Start Small

1. "Guy Starts Dance Party," YouTube, accessed December 28, 2015,  bit.ly/DGSDance and bit.ly/DGSParty.
2. Hui-yong Yu, "Self-Storage Magnates Cash In on the Surge in Real Estate," *Bloomberg Business*, August 6, 2008, accessed December 28, 2015, http://www.bloomberg.com/news/articles/2014–08–06/self-storage-magnates-cash-in-on-the-surge-in-real-estate.
3. Self Storage Association, Products and Services, http://www.selfstorage.org//products-services/product-info-/producted/12ssds4870.
4. Please don't stop sending checks.


## Conclusion: As Good as It Gets

1. United Nations, "We Can End Poverty: Millennium Development and Goals beyond 2015," accessed December 28, 2015, http://www.un.org/millenniumgoals/poverty.shtml.

*Looking for a simple way to Do Good?*

Throw a Garage Sale for Orphans party to SELL your excess. GIVE the money to a project or HON community of your choice, and HELP that local leader make a difference for orphans, vulnerable children, and struggling families in his or her community.

*Do Good.*
*Do Good Well.*
*Do Good Together.*

Visit
www.helponenow.org/garage-sale-for-orphans
for more information.

Help One Now seeks to gather normal, everyday folks into a tribe of people who are dedicated to using their gifts, talents, and resources to empower high-capacity local leaders to serve orphans, vulnerable children, and needy families in their communities.

*One Leader.*
*One Child.*
*One Community.*

Find out more at
www.helponenow.com.